GW00472325

Books III

The Life of
St. Philip Neri

By Fr. Pietro Giacomo Bacci

Edited by William R. Bloomfield

†

Published by Bloomfield Books
www.SacredArtSeries.com

†

March 2017

†

ISBN: 9781520765709

Cover Art: St. Philip Neri in Ecstasy, by Guido Reni (1615)

Preface

The Life of St. Philip Neri by Fr. Pietro Giacomo Bacci was published in 1622, just 27 years after St. Philip's death in 1595. Fr. Bacci was a member of the Roman Oratory, the Congregation founded by St. Philip, and he based his book on the Processes instituted for St. Philip's canonization. These Processes began just two months after Philip's death and depended on sworn testimony from hundreds of witnesses to Philip's extraordinary virtue and his many miracles. The Processes led to Philip's beatification in 1615—also the year Guido Reni completed his famous painting (see cover) that hangs over Philip's tomb at Chiesa Nuova in Rome—and ultimately his canonization in 1622.

While there have been many books written on St. Philip Neri, Fr. Bacci's book is a classic that has been translated into many languages and republished numerous times in the hundreds of years since St. Philip's death. In republishing Fr. Bacci's *The Life of St. Philip Neri* for Kindle, it is my intention to increase access to this fine work. Ultimately, it is my hope that we may all learn to imitate St. Philip's deep love of God and neighbor.

This paperback edition of *The Life of St. Philip Neri* is based on the 1902 revised edition of Fr. Frederick Ignatius Antrobus of the London Oratory. Minor adjustments to spelling and punctuation have been made where appropriate. As appendices to this edition, I have included both the 1902 preface and 1794 preface, both of which provide background on Fr. Bacci's book.

The Life of St. Philip Neri includes six books. This second volume contains books three and four. It is my intention to publish all six books in both Kindle and paperback editions.

William R. Bloomfield
Lansing, Michigan
March 6, 2017

Table of Contents

Book III: Which treats of the gifts God vouchsafed to him

Chapter 1 – Philip's raptures and ecstasies

Philip's great and solid virtues, which we have related in the preceding book, were crowned and adorned by the Divine Majesty with various gifts and graces. The Lord was not contented with having raised him to this height of charity, and given him so remarkable a spirit of prayer. It was his good pleasure to exalt him to penetrate the ineffable secrets of the Divine Greatness in wonderful ecstasies and raptures, which were of frequent occurrence during the whole of his life; although, out of humility, he used every means and tried every artifice to avoid them, even doing violence to himself for that end.

In consequence of an important cause, which they had at that time before the Pope, the Dominican fathers had the devotion of the Forty Hours at their convent of the Minerva, and Philip, together with Francesco Maria Tarugi and some others, was there by invitation. While he was kneeling in one of the remotest parts of the church, praying fervently, he fell all at once into an ecstasy, and remained with his eyes fixed on the Blessed Sacrament, his face slightly smiling, and the rest of his body perfectly motionless. The prior, Fra. Angelo Diaceti, who was afterwards bishop of Fiesole, and a great friend of Philip, noticed it, and in company with another friar went to him, and called him several times; they then touched him, and found him as cold as ice. Thinking that some accident had happened to him, they carried him to a cell in the novitiate, where, after he had remained a long while in that state, he returned to himself, and cried out, "Victory! Victory! Our prayer is heard." The prior, in great astonishment, begged him earnestly to explain the cause of the change that had come over him, and what that victory was of which he spoke. The Saint at first made a great difficulty of explaining anything; but at last, being prevailed upon by the prior's reiterated petitions, he said, "Well, the business for which we have had this devotion has succeeded, and we have been heard." When he was questioned more narrowly about his ecstasy, he said that he had seen Jesus Christ in the consecrated host, giving benediction with His most holy hand to all those who were present at the devotion; and that they should therefore thank God for the victory they had gained. It was observed, that at the very moment in which the Saint returned to himself, the Pope had given sentence in favor of the Dominicans, in the cause for which they had exposed the Blessed Sacrament, and had the devotion of the Forty Hours.

Fabrizio de' Massimi, going one morning to confession to him, found the door of his room closed; and opening it very softly, he saw the Saint in the act of praying, raised upon his feet, his eyes looking to heaven, and his hands uplifted, and making many gestures. He stood for a while watching him, and then going close to him, he saluted him. The Saint, although he had his face towards him, so that he could easily see him, and could not naturally have avoided seeing him, did in fact neither see him nor return him any answer. Fabrizio, struck with this, looked at him again, feeling himself no little devotion from simply beholding Philip in this state of abstraction, which lasted about eight minutes longer. When Philip came to himself and perceived that Fabrizio was present, he asked him how he had got in; he replied, that he had not found the door bolted; whereupon, without another word, the Saint heard his confession. Francesco della Molara also going one morning to confession to him, found the door open, and the Saint sitting praying. Francesco knelt down before him to confess, when he perceived that the servant of God was in an ecstasy, and it was a quarter of an hour before he came to himself.

Another time he was in the chapel of the Visitation, one of his favorite haunts, because he was particularly fond of Barocci's picture which is there; and sitting down, according to his custom, upon a little seat, he passed unawares into a most sweet ecstasy. Some women, his penitents, who were at no great distance, saw this, and went up to him, and after having looked at him for a while, they called him, and shook him so vehemently that he came to himself. But Philip, disliking of all things to be observed when enjoying these divine favors, got up, and began to cry out, and call Father Antonio to send those women away, because they were annoying him, and would not let him alone; and he pretended to be in a violent passion; and all this was merely an artifice to destroy the good opinion they might have formed of him from finding him in an ecstasy.

Paolo Ricuperati, a prelate of both the Segnature, and one of the holy father's familiar friends, went one evening to confession to him at San Girolamo, and found him at supper with Messer Giovanni Animuccia. Philip rose from table and heard his confession, and in putting his hands on his head to give him absolution, went into an ecstasy and remained motionless. He remained in this state for a considerable time, to the astonishment of the prelate and Animuccia, who was also an eye-witness of it; and when at last he came to himself, he gave him absolution: and the like happened to many other of his penitents, as the time of the hearing of confessions was frequently to him the time of these heavenly favors.

About the year 1585, Father Antonio Gallonio found Philip in bed one morning apparently almost dead. The medical men were immediately summoned; they applied a hot iron to his head, blisters to his arms, and other remedies to the shoulders. Nothing, however, seemed to rouse him, or do him any good; and F. Giovan Francesco Bordino gave him Extreme Unction; but one of the fathers saying "Credo, Credo," the Saint came to himself, and said in an audible voice, "What Credo, Credo is this?" and then opened his eyes, looked round on all of them weeping; and when some of them said, "Father, you have been very ill," he answered, "Nay, I have had no other illness than the one you have provided me with." They found afterwards that it was no fit, but an ecstasy; and it was perhaps because of these frequent ecstasies that he used repeatedly to say in bidding them good night after he was in bed, "Go away, and if you find me dead tomorrow morning, bury me." At mass his ecstasies were frequent, as we learn from those who served, and especially Cardinal Ottavio Paravicino, who, when young, served the Saint's mass for twenty years, though not continuously. He also found it so difficult to prevent himself going into an ecstasy, when he was in the presence of the Pope, because of the interior movements which it caused in his heart, that whenever he was going to see his Holiness he used to say to the fathers, "Now pray for me, that I may not commit some foolery or other."

He was often seen with his whole body raised in the air; and among others Paolo Sfondrato, Cardinal of S. Cecilia, saw him in prayer raised several spans from the ground, indeed almost to the ceiling, as he told Paul V a little time before he died. Giovanni Battista Modio was on one occasion so grievously ill, that his death was hourly expected, and he had already lost his speech and senses. At this juncture the holy father came to visit him, as he was a friend of the family. He stayed a little while with him, and then retired into a solitary room to pray for him. When midnight was passed some of those who were attending the sick man began to wonder where Philip had retired, and they found him with his body raised entirely up into the air, and with rays of glory all around him. When they saw him in this state, they cried out, "Come here quickly, come here quickly;" and all the attendants, hearing, ran to the spot, and they saw him raised from the ground to such a height that his head almost touched the ceiling, while a glory of rays shone all round him. In about half an hour Philip came to himself, and went to the invalid in great joy, and laying his hand on his head, said to him, "Keep up your heart, you will not die;" at that instant the power of speech returned to the sick man, and he began to converse with the Saint on various topics as distinctly as if he had not been ill at all, and in a few days he had entirely recovered.

Father Gregorio Ozes, the Dominican, declared that before he entered religion he also had seen Philip raised in the air, and with a resplendent light around him. But the Saint was not only seen raised in this manner in private places, or by one or few persons at once; even in churches and public places he was, against his own will and endeavors, carried off into these ecstasies. On one occasion he was praying in S. Peter's, at the tombs of the apostles, and his whole body was seen to rise all at once into the air, and with his clothes gathered up, as they had been when he was kneeling, and then to descend with equal suddenness; while he, fearing lest he should have been observed, fled away with the utmost rapidity. The same thing happened in many other churches, so that when he entered a church in company with others, he used to stay a very little time, but merely say a Pater and an Ave, and then rise from his knees, to prevent the possibility of his going into an ecstasy.

When he was saying mass he was repeatedly raised into the air, and several persons took particular notice of it. At Torre di Specehi some of the nuns saw him three or four palms above the ground during mass; and a little girl, who was at his mass at San Girolamo, saw him about two palms from the ground, and turning to her mother said with childish simplicity, "Mother, I think that father there is possessed with a bad spirit; look at him, how he stays in the air!" but the mother replied, "Hold your tongue, it is a Saint in an ecstasy." Sulpizia Sirleti, one of his penitents, seeing him raised into the air on one occasion, said within herself, "Surely this father is possessed, else he would never stay in the air in this way." Going afterwards to confession to him, she was ashamed to mention this suspicion to the Saint, and began, "Father, I have said," and then stopped, not having courage to finish her sentence. But Philip said to her, "Go on, you silly creature; you have been finding fault with me, eh? that is it, is it not?" She said it was, and he asked her further what it was; Sulpizia answered, "The other morning, when your Reverence was saying mass, and was raised above the ground" - Philip hearing this much put his finger on his mouth and said, "Hush, hush;" but she added, "Then I said in my heart, O dear! this father is possessed." At these words Philip burst out laughing, and repeated several times, interruptedly, in his usual way, "True, I am possessed."

Sometimes when he was saying mass he was seen with rays of glory round his head. In the first year of the pontificate of Sixtus V, Aurelio

Bacci, a Sienese, saw Philip saying mass at the high altar of our church, and as soon as he began the Memento of the Living, he saw him with a splendor round his head, of the color of gold, but more gleaming, about four fingers wide all round, and in the shape of a diadem. Aurelio, thinking it might perhaps be some defect in his own vision, turned himself several times in order to change the point of view, and then looked again, but still he saw the same thing distinctly. He rubbed his eyes with his hands and his pocket handkerchief, and looking at the heads of other people he saw nothing of the kind, but turning again to Philip, he saw the glory as plain as before, and it lasted until the holy father had communicated.

Another time when he was saying mass at San Girolamo, a little girl about twelve years old, saw him raised in the air, and surrounded by a most white and resplendent cloud, which covered him all over; and although his vestments were red, or of some other color, not white, yet he appeared all white and shining, and remained in this for half a quarter of an hour; and this same thing happened more than once. Muzio Achillei, a priest of San Severino, and Philip's penitent, also saw the Saint saying mass with his face shining like bright gold.

When Vincenzo Lanteri, the Archbishop of Ragusa, was young, Philip used to pull his hair and box his ears whenever he met him; and one day Vincenzo, meeting him in the street, and fearing lest he should do the same in public, determined to be beforehand with him, and going up to him, took his hand and kissed it reverently; and in taking it he perceived it all gold color, and shining with rays that seemed to come from the middle of it. Wondering whether this could come from any natural cause, he looked about him, and saw that the air was thick, and no sunshine to be seen anywhere; full of wonder and perplexity, he went immediately to Chiesa Nuova, and related the whole matter to Father Tommaso Bozzio, who confirmed him in his belief that it was supernatural, and told him that many had seen Philip's hand as it were all of gold. But to relate all the matters of this kind, with his ecstasies and raptures, would only weary the reader, both from the sameness and the number of the instances.

Chapter 2 – Philip's visions

Besides these ecstasies and ravishments of spirit, Philip was favored with many visions and apparitions; indeed they were so frequent that they occurred almost every night. A few only shall be related here, sufficient to show the reader how this glorious Saint, whose mind and heart were continually in heaven, was favored by God with heavenly visits and unearthly consolations.

On one occasion before he was ordained priest, or had come to any determination about a state of life, he was praying with particular fervor, that he might know the will of God about it. It was in the morning just at sunrise, and as he was praying, the glorious precursor of Christ, S. John the Baptist, appeared to him. He was so filled with devotion at this apparition, that the usual trembling came over him, and after he had remained in rapture for some time, the vision disappeared, leaving him in great spiritual fervor and most burning love; and from certain things in the apparition, he told Cardinal Frederic Borromeo that he gathered it to be the will of God that he should live in Rome for the good of others in poverty, and a special detachment from everything. The same thing was signified to him in another vision which he had of two blessed souls, while he was at prayer.

One of them had a hard roll in his hand, which he appeared to be eating without any other food. Philip seeing this, and wishing to know the meaning of it, heard those words, "God wishes that you should live in the middle of Rome, as if you were in a desert, abstaining from eating flesh, so far as may be allowable for you." This he observed perseveringly to the day of his death, eating meat very seldom, and then rather out of condescension to the will of others, or because of illness; otherwise he used to abstain from it, assigning as a reason that it did not agree with him. These visions, in addition to what Father Agostino Ghettini of the Tre Fontane said to him, and which we have already narrated, put Philip's mind completely at ease regarding his state of life, and filled him with an inward contentment and clearness of mind which never left him during the whole course of his life.

Another time, after he was a priest, he was praying on Christmas night with Costanzo Tassone, and Sebastiano, the musician whom we have spoken of before; and in the fervor of his prayer he saw Christ appear upon the altar in the form of a child; whereupon, turning to his companions, he said, "Do you not see Christ the Child upon the altar?" They answered, "No;" and he, perceiving that the favor was granted to him only, held his peace and went on with his prayer. Once as when he was saying mass, Cesare Tomasi of Ripatransona, his penitent, observed that at the elevation, after he had laid the host down, he remained a long time as in ecstasy before the elevation of the chalice; and that after mass he returned to the sacristy with a joyous and smiling countenance. Cesare afterwards asked him why he had been so long at the elevation, and why he had come back into the sacristy so joyous; the Saint laid his hand on his head and smiled, but gave him no answer; but his penitent growing importunate, and asking him over and over again, Philip at last reluctantly told him that sometimes at mass after the consecration, God was pleased to show him the glory of Paradise in a vision; but he begged him not to tell this to anyone else.

He had also the consolation of seeing the souls of many, and particularly of his friends and penitents, go into heaven. Mario Tosini, one of the first of the company of the Santissima Trinità, a man of singular goodness, and whose life has been written by Bonsignor Cacciaguerra, appeared to Philip immediately after his death, about midnight, and in great joy. He called twice with a loud voice, "Philip, Philip," and the Saint, lifting his eyes to heaven, saw the soul of Mario, all bright and resplendent, enter into Paradise. The following morning he heard the news of his death, and found upon inquiry, that he had expired at the very hour the vision appeared. The Saint himself related this to some of his spiritual children, when conversing with them about the goodness of that servant of God, and he said that human language could never express the beauty of a justified soul.

Vincenzo Miniatore, also one of the first brothers of the Santissima Trinità, and his penitent, a man of great perfection, appeared to him immediately after his death, all glorious, and Philip saw him ascend to heaven surrounded with splendor. In the morning he went to console the widow, and said to her, "Your husband knocked at my door last night and recommended you and all your family to my care; you need be under no uneasiness about him; he is gone to Paradise;" and from that time the holy father always assisted the family in its necessities, as has been mentioned elsewhere.

Marco Antonio Corteselli of Como, cashier of the bank of the Cevoli, one of his spiritual children, the most dear to him, and a man very much given to prayer and works of mercy, and who for many years transacted the business of the Capuchins for them, passed to a better life and the Saint went with Father Antonio Gallonio and another priest to see his body which was in Santa Caterina close to S. Girolamo della Carità. After having looked at it for a long time with great attention, he made a painter take a portrait of it; the priest wondering at this, Gallonio told him he need not be surprised, for that Philip had said, "The soul of Corteselli appeared to me last night all luminous, and remained conversing with me for about four or five hours, and after that was borne up to heaven by angels, and his presence filled the whole room with a resplendent brightness." Corteselli had as great an esteem for Philip, as Philip for him, and talking one day with Paolo Maji, a priest, and procurator of the Sacred Penitentiary, he said of Philip, as if in the spirit of prophecy, "Messer Paolo, this good father is not known, and some think him an ordinary man; but he will be well known when he is dead."

Fabrizio de' Massimi had a daughter about thirteen years old, whose name was Elena. This child was most fervent in the love of Christ, and most obedient to her director in the least particular; she wept bitterly over our Lord's Passion, communicated at least three times a week, and that with abundance of tears, and had such a relish and appetite for prayer, that it seemed like the very food that sustained her. She had a mean opinion of herself, preferring everyone to herself, and she had an extreme desire to suffer, that she might in some measure be conformed to our Savior's Passion. In her last illness, when Baronius took her the holy communion, after she had communicated, she saw Jesus Christ shedding His Precious Blood into her soul; and at last, having already foreseen her death, she passed away to heaven with signs of the greatest devotion. No sooner had she breathed her last, than Philip heard the angels singing, and saw them, as he himself told Baronius, carrying the little virgin's soul to Paradise as they sang, and Baronius says the Saint called it a "Hebrew song."

In fact, those who were most intimate with Philip, held it for certain, that none of his spiritual children died without his being certified of the state of their souls. Besides the apparitions already mentioned, the same happened at the deaths of Lavinia de' Rustici, the first wife of Fabrizio de' Massimi, of Sister Elena and Sister Scholastica, her daughters, who were at Torre di Specchi, of Patrizio Patrizi, and of Virgilio Crescenzi; for consoling the sons of this last, he said, "Do not make yourselves unhappy; your father is in Paradise, and I tell you that I know it," and He repeated these words several times over. Many other instances of a like nature might be mentioned; and Cardinal Frederic Borromeo says, that Philip in talking with him about this very matter, spoke of it as an ordinary and usual thing with him; and it was so well known that God had given him this gift of knowing the condition of departed souls, especially of his own penitents, that Father Giovanni Antonio Lucci, when his mother was dead, begged him to pray that he might know the state of her soul; and Philip after his prayer said, "Be of good cheer; your mother is in heaven," and Giovanni hearing this wept in the joy of his heart. He told him the same of his father when he died, and giving him the reason, said, "Because the same thing has happened as in the case of my own father's death;" whence we may gather, that Philip's father had gone to heaven, and we may believe this to be owing to the prayers and merit of such a son. Whenever conversation turned on the beauty of souls, he used to speak as a man would do who was accustomed to such visions, and it was a common phrase with him, "it is impossible to describe the beauty of a soul that has died in the grace of the Lord."

We have already had several times to mention Giovanni Animuccia, one of the Saint's spiritual children, a musician and chapel master at S. Peter's, who used to go every day to the Oratory to sing after the sermons, taking several other singers with him. He was a man of such purity, that after he had put himself under Philip's direction, he lived with his wife as though she had been his sister. During his life he was extremely harassed by scruples; but in his last sickness it pleased God to free him from them entirely, so that he died in the greatest peace and joyfulness. One evening, about three years after his death, about an hour before the Ave, when the sermons were over, he appeared to a certain Alfonso, a Portuguese, and a friend of his, and asked him if the Oratory was finished. His friend replied that it was, forgetting at the moment that Animuccia was dead. Animuccia added, "I beg you will speak to Father Philip, and ask him to pray for me," and then disappeared. The Portuguese, reflecting, remembered that his friend had been dead a good while since, and immediately returned to the place where he had seen the apparition, but all had disappeared whereupon he went to the Saint in great fear, and told him what had happened. Philip the next morning made him relate the whole vision in the Oratory, in the presence of all, and then sent to different churches to have masses said for the soul of the deceased, besides having a solemn requiem sung at San Giovanni of the Florentines. Afterwards he said to the brothers at the Oratory, "Animuccia has arrived," meaning, that he had gone from purgatory to Paradise.

In some instances he was allowed to see the beauty of souls, even while they were united to the body. Speaking of S. Ignatius, the founder of the Company of Jesus, he said that the intense beauty of that holy man was such and so great, that he could discern it in his countenance, and he declared that he had seen rays of glory issue from his face. So high was the opinion which Philip had of him, that after his death, in case of any special need, he used to go to his tomb, and recommend himself to him, although he was not yet canonized, and he obtained by this means whatever he asked; and when he read his life, he said several times, "How many things are left out, how many more than are written! O if all had been registered, how would men's admiration for Ignatius have increased!"

He declared he had observed the same thing in looking at S. Charles, and that he had seen him beautiful and resplendent as an angel. He saw also a great splendor in the countenance of one of his youthful penitents, named Giovanni Battista Saraceni of Collescepoli, who afterwards became a Dominican and was called Fra. Pietro Martire; and by his virtue and abilities he was raised to the chief offices of his religion, and was created Vicar General of the order, ending his edifying life by a most holy death. He also saw at different times some Carthusian monks with their faces shining, as they came from prayer.

Philip, however, had not only visions of good spirits for his own consolation, but of evil ones also for the exercise of his virtue, and the instruction of others. When he was living at S. Girolamo, he ordered Father Giovanni Antonio Lucci to exorcise a woman who was possessed, and in contempt of the devil to give her several blows. The evil spirit was so enraged at this, that he appeared to Philip the next night in a most brutal form, in order to frighten him, and in going away left such a stench in the room that the Saint smelled it for a long time afterwards. One day he was in the Oratory at San Girolamo, when, besides the brothers, Gabriello Palleotto, who was afterwards cardinal, was there. They were conversing of the things of God, when all on a sudden Philip rose and said, "My brothers, behold here is the devil; kneel down and pray." He himself immediately went down on his knees, and making the sign of the cross in front of himself, he said to the devil,

"Thou shalt not enter;" whereupon the evil one disappeared instantly from the eyes of the Saint, and they pursued their exercises in peace.

Another time he was in the baths of Diocletian, close to Santa Maria degli Angeli, and he saw above one of the monuments of antiquity, which there are there, the devil in the form of a young man; and looking fixedly at him, he observed that he changed his countenance, and appeared sometimes younger, sometimes older, sometimes ugly, and sometimes beautiful. Perceiving that the devil was doing this in order to delude him, he commanded him in the name of God to depart; upon which he immediately vanished, leaving a most horrible stench behind him. This stench was always like sulphur, and although he only smelled it in general, yet sometimes others perceived it also; as was the case one morning when he laid his hand on the head of a possessed person; such a pestilential smell was left upon his hand, that although he washed it with soap, and different sweet-scented things, the stench lasted for several days. During this time he gave his hand to several persons to smell, in order that they might take occasion from it to avoid sin more carefully; as he declared it came from the devil, by whom that poor woman was harassed and possessed. Upon another occasion when Philip was in our church, the devil appeared to him in the form of a boy of six or seven years of age, who held a pocket handkerchief to his mouth, and made game of Philip. The Saint looking severely at him, drove him away; and asking Gallonio, who was there, if he had seen that boy, he added, "It was the devil who came unto the church to do some mischief, either to make someone fall into sin, or because some great sinner has entered the church."

In a word, so bitter was the devil's hatred to Philip, that if he prayed or performed any action at all of a religious nature, he almost always endeavored to disturb him and weary him. One night when the Saint was praying, he appeared to him with a terrible aspect, in order to frighten him, but Philip invoking the Queen of heaven, the evil one instantly disappeared. Another time when the Saint had retired to a sort of little balcony above his room, the demon, not being able to do him any other mischief, stained his clothes all over with dirt; another time in order to annoy him, he upset a table upon him and when the Saint was ill, the devil used often to put out the light which was kept burning in the room. Besides this, he was continually making a noise in the room; so that Gallonio, who slept underneath, was frequently obliged to rise and go upstairs to see what the meaning of the noise was, and never found anything: but Philip repeatedly said to him, "The devil has tried to frighten me tonight, but I recommended myself to the most holy Mary, and she delivered me."

Philip, as well by the sanctity of his life, as by his experience, had acquired great discernment in these matters, and knew well how to distinguish true from false visions. He was very particular every time that conversation turned upon them, whether speculatively or practically, to warn men against being deluded, which is very easy and probable; and for this end he constantly quoted that common doctrine of the holy fathers, that we ought not ordinarily to give credit to visions; and although he was favored by God with such lights and elevations of mind, yet he did not at all like ecstasies or visions in public; for he said they were most dangerous things, and that we ought to seek for spiritual sweetnesses and consolations, and keep them as secret as possible. He also said that visions, as well good as bad, were wont to come even to those who did not wish for them, and therefore that no person could confidently say, "I do not desire these things, and so I shall not be exposed to delusions or to visions," but that there is need of great humility, great resignation and detachment, to prevent our leaving God because of visions. He used to add that it was a difficult thing to receive visions, and not be puffed up by them, more difficult not to think ourselves worthy of them, but the most difficult of all to think ourselves actually unworthy, and to prefer patience, obedience, and humility, to the sweetness of visions. He taught that the visions which were not useful either to the person who received them, or to the Church in general, were in no way to be esteemed, and that real visions begin by breeding horror and fear, but leave behind them great peace and tranquility, whereas counterfeit visions work just in a contrary way. He warned confessors never to trust to the revelations of their spiritual children, and particularly of women, because they seem sometimes to be far advanced in spirituality, but more often than not it all melts away, and many have made shipwreck of themselves in following after these things. He counselled, therefore, nay, in many instances commanded his spiritual children to reject such things with all their might, and not to fear that in doing so they should displease the Divine Majesty, because this is one of the very tests to distinguish true from false visions. One day when he mounted into the pulpit to preach, he spoke against those who gave easy credence to visions, raptures, and ecstasies, and said, "I know a person present here who can go into an ecstasy whenever he pleases, God having among other graces granted him this also, but a person ought to fly from such things and. to hide them;" when he had said this he felt himself being carried away in spirit; whereupon he strove to the best of his power to hinder himself from going into an ecstasy, and being unable to proceed with his sermon, he leaned with his hand upon his knee, and said, "He who wishes for ecstasies and visions, does not know what he desires! O if everybody did but know what an ecstasy is!" and then bursting into tears, he came down from the pulpit, and went away.

Another time when Fr. Giovan Francesco Bordini had been discoursing upon ecstasies, after he had finished, Philip mounted the pulpit and said, that as that father had spoken of ecstasies, he wished to add a word or two to the discourse; "I have known," said he, a woman of holy life who had continual ecstasies for a long time, and then God took them from her: now I ask you, when do you think I esteemed that woman more, when she had ecstasies, or when she had not? I tell you, that to my mind, she was without comparison more estimable when she had not ecstasies than when she had;" and with these words he came down from the pulpit and went away. On one occasion he was told that our Lord frequently appeared, and S. Catherine of Siena almost continually, to a virgin of the third order of S. Dominic. He replied, as one who had had much experience in such matters, "Women very easily deceive themselves; tell her, therefore, when such visions come, to spit in their face, and be the persons who they may to make no esteem of them, and not only not to desire them, but to despise them." The virgin acted upon this advice, and kept herself always in a prudent fear of being deceived, to the immense profit of her soul.

We have already mentioned Francesco Maria, commonly surnamed Il Ferrarese, one of the Saint's first spiritual children. One night the devil appeared to him in the form of the Blessed Virgin, with much splendor. In the morning Francesco told Philip of it, but he answered, "This is the devil, and not the Virgin; if he returns again, spit in his face." The following night the same vision returned; Francesco spit in his face, and the demon immediately disappeared. Francesco continued his prayer, and presently the most holy Virgin came to him in reality; he wished to spit at her, but she said, "Spit if you can." He tried to do so, but found his mouth and tongue so dry and parched, that he could not. Our Blessed Lady told him he had done well to perform the obedience which had been given him, and then disappeared, leaving him full of consolation and joyousness of spirit.

Antonio Fucci, the physician of whom we have spoken before, attended a nun of a holy life, who was seriously ill, and finding her one day lost in divine contemplation, he waited till she came to herself, when turning immediately to him she said, "O how beautiful have I seen you just now in Paradise." Antonio, hearing these words, and reflecting on them, went to confer with the holy father, and on the same day fell ill. His indisposition continually increasing, the enemy of human nature, in order to delude him, came to visit him several times under the guise of a physician, promising him a long life, and telling him that he would certainly not die of that sickness. He mentioned this to the Saint, who came to him every day; Philip told him this was not the physician, but the devil; and Antonio, discovering the delusion, resigned himself to the will of God, and died a holy death a few days afterwards. The Saint used to relate this, in order to impress upon his children, that those who are in danger of death ought not to credit visions readily, especially when a promise of long life was made in them, because they are generally delusions of the devil, who wishes a man to die still hoping for life, and so without due preparation; and he used to say, that the danger of rejecting true visions, was much less than that of putting trust in false ones.

Mattia Maffei, a priest, and one of the Saint's penitents, having been miraculously cured of an illness by him, the night following had a dream, which shall be related for the sake of the meaning it contains. It seemed to this good priest, that he was conducted by the holy father into a most spacious meadow, where there was an innumerable multitude of princes, richly and superbly clothed; and while he was looking, in one instant the whole scene sank down, and everything turned into flames and fire, and an immense number of devils appeared. He remained standing on a very narrow edge of the meadow, and one of the devils with some hooks tried all he could to pull him into the fire, and while he was defending himself, the Saint looked at him and smiled. At last he took him by the hand and said to him, "Come, Mattia; do not be afraid," and he led him through the midst of a tangled thicket of exceedingly sharp thorns: the Saint himself seemed to be unhurt by them, but he dragged Maffei through them in such a way as to give him the most acute pain. He then led him into an inmost beautiful meadow, at the end of which there was a most beautiful hill, and at the foot of it three angels in shining garments, one with a cross in his hand, and the other two with two candlesticks and lighted candles, and behind them was an immense multitude of virgins, widows, and married women, many of whom made an obeisance to the holy father, and many asked Maffei if he wished to go with them; but he not daring to speak, the Saint answered for him, saying that it was not time yet, because he was not altogether a good man. All this multitude passed through a wide alley, with trees in blossom on both sides, on which were little angels, who kept breaking branches off, and throwing them down on the crowd below, and singing all the while most sweetly, *"Gloria in excelsis Deo,"* and the hymn, *"Jesu corona Virginum."* At last when the multitude reached the top of the hill, they entered into a most beautiful palace; and when all had entered, Maffei awoke, and so the dream ended. He went immediately to confession to the Saint, and before he had spoken a word, Philip asked him if he believed in dreams; and Maffei wishing to lay hold of this opportunity to relate his dream, the Saint with a severe and menacing look cut him short, and said, "Get away with you; he who wishes to go to Paradise must be an honest man and a good Christian, and not a believer in dreams."

In fine, this was the doctrine that he was continually preaching - that we must catch by the feet those who wish to fly without wings, and drag them down to the ground by main force, lest they should fall into the devil's net - meaning those who go after visions, dreams, and the like, forgetting that we must always walk along the road of mortification of our own passions, and of holy humility.

Chapter 3 – Of Philip's gift of prophecy; and first of his predicting the deaths of several persons

To the gift of visions, Philip joined that of prophecy; indeed he was specially eminent even among other Saints in this gift, as well in predicting future events, as in seeing absent things, and in reading the secrets of hearts. If all the examples of this which it would be easy to adduce were narrated, they would fill entire volumes, as many of the witnesses affirmed in the processes; and in truth the Congregation of Rites pronounced that in this gift of prophecy, *non est inventus similis illi*, none was found like him. It will be sufficient, therefore, to give a few specimens, from which it may be gathered how singularly he was favored by God in this respect; and we will begin with the predictions he made of the deaths of others.

Costanzo Tassone, who has been mentioned before, was called from Milan to Rome, by S. Pius V, and when he arrived there, went at once to dismount at S. Girolamo della Carità. One of Philip's penitents was at the window that looks into the piazza; he immediately ran to the Saint and said, "Father, here is Messer Costanzo." Philip immediately ordered Ottavio Paravicino and Germanico Fedeli, who were both youths at that time, to stretch themselves like corpses over the threshold of the door through which Costanzo had to pass. They obeyed, and Tassone, seeing the two youths stretched in this way on the ground, was a little disturbed, and begged them to let him pass; but they remained in that position till Philip caused them to rise, and Costanzo ran to embrace him. In a short time he fell sick, and was dead within the fortnight.

Giovan Angelo Crivelli went to confess to the Saint on Holy Thursday; he was perfectly well at the time, but Philip looking earnestly into his face, said to him, "My Giovan Angelo, prepare yourself, go and pray a little while before the crucifix in the church of San Girolamo, and then come back, for God wants something of you." Crivelli answered,

"May His Divine Majesty do what seems best to Him; for I am ready to receive anything from His hand." "But," rejoined the Saint, "if it were to please God to send you a very grievous tribulation, would you bear it willingly?" "Trusting in His aid," said he, "I would bear it most willingly." "Well then," replied Philip, "see that you are prepared, for at Easter God will call you." Giovan Angelo went away, and that same evening a fever came on, and on the fourth day he died and the Saint said afterwards to Giovan's daughter, that her father was gone to Paradise.

One morning he called Francesco della Molara to him suddenly, and said to him, "What would you do, Francesco, if your wife were to die?" "Indeed, father," replied he, "I do not know." "Well now," said Philip, "think on what you would do if your wife were to die." Fulvia de' Cavalieri, as Francesco's wife was called, was at that time both young and well, and with no appearance of illness about her, but in ten days she was seized with a malignant fever, and died within the fortnight.

Girolamo Cordella, a physician of some reputation and a friend of the Saint, was appointed physician to the court, but continued, notwithstanding, to go about Rome visiting his patients whereupon the Saint said, "This will last but a short time; he wishes to return to his old labors, and he will die." Soon afterwards Cordella was taken ill, and his wife sent some one to the Saint to let him know that her husband was ill, and to beg his prayers. Father Gallonio went downstairs to see who it was that was asking for Philip, and what they wanted. As soon as he was gone the Saint began to say, "O poor Cordella! Ah! this time he will die without fail; his hour is come." Those who were present wondered at these words, for Father Gallonio had not yet returned with the news of his illness. But when he came back, and delivered the message of Cordella's wife, the Saint again said, "O poor Cordella! the course of his life is finished; he will die presently." Those who were there said, "Well, father, if we cannot mend his body, we may at least help his soul." Philip replied in his usual manner, "Yes, this we can do, certainly, this we can do." The eighth day of Cordella's illness came, and very early in the morning, Father Gallonio and Consolini taking a light to the Saint, he said, "Cordella died at such an hour, did he not?" but perceiving that they knew nothing about it, he immediately turned the conversation to something else. He afterwards sent them to see how matters stood, and they found that Cordella had died at the very hour that Philip had named; and Philip himself said afterwards to Cardinal Agostino Cusano, "I was present at Girolamo Cordella's death, although I was in my own room all the while."

Orintia, the wife of Pompeo Colonna, was a lady, who to the distinction of noble birth added that of eminent piety. She constantly visited the hospital of San Giacomo of the Incurables, in order to succor those poor patients in soul as well as in body. At last she fell ill, and was attended by the principal physicians of Rome, who said that her indisposition was not of any importance. But Orintia, putting no confidence in the medical men, sent to ask Philip to visit her. He went, and conversed with her for a long time upon spiritual matters; before bidding her goodbye, he dipped his finger in holy water, made the sign of the cross upon her, and urging her to call to mind the passion of our Savior, he departed. In going out of the palace he met the physicians, and when he said that the lady was very ill, they ridiculed him. Then Philip replied, "Well, you may laugh at me now, but I tell you that on such a day, (mentioning the day,) she will pass to another world." At these words the physicians burst out laughing; but on the day mentioned Orintia died.

Elena Cibi fell sick, together with her husband Domenico Mazzei; and Tamiria Cevoli, Elena's mother, fearing from the symptoms of their complaint that both her daughter and her son-in-law would die, went to the Saint to recommend them to his prayers. "Father," said she, "I fear that both of them will die." "No," replied the Saint, "no, one is enough;" and so it was, for Domenico died, and Elena got well, and leaving the cares of the world, she became a nun in the convent of San Vincenzo, at Prato in Tuscany. Vittoria Cibi, Elena's sister, went to the Saint to confess; he asked her how long it was since she had visited her sister who was a nun at Torre di Speech, called Sister Vincenza. Vittoria replied that it was several days since; "Well then," answered the Saint, "go and see her every day, for she will die very shortly." Not long afterwards the nun, who was in perfect health, and of a strong constitution, was suddenly attacked by a malignant fever, and died in eighteen days.

Marcello Ferro wished to leave Rome with Cardinal Gambara; but the holy father told him not to go, because his father, Alfonso Ferro, would die in a few days. Marcello obeyed, and although his father was strong and well, he died at the end of twenty days. Alessandro Crescenzi went to the Saint on the 1st of August, 1594, in excellent bodily health; and Philip, as soon as he saw him, said, "Get ready, for in a short time you will die;" and on the 16th of the same month Alessandro expired. Guglielmo, the brother of Giovan Francesco Bucca, fell ill, and Philip said to Giovan Francesco, "Your brother will die, and do not fret about it, for it is well for him that he should die now;" and his death took place accordingly. A clerk of the Congregation, named Leonardo, a person of exemplary life, was ill, and the Saint was asked to pray for him, that he might not die. But Philip, having withdrawn for a while, returned and told Antonio Gallonio that he would rather not make that prayer, perhaps because he knew that death would be better than health for Leonardo, who did in fact die of that illness.

Virgilio Crescenzi fell ill, and as his indisposition was at first very slight, his family never dreamed of his dying. The Saint, however, went to visit him, and told Costanza his wife that she must acquiesce in what was pleasing to God. On hearing this she was very much disturbed; but knowing the favors which God daily granted through Philip to those who recommended themselves to his prayers, she drew him aside, and shedding floods of tears, she knelt down before him, and earnestly besought him to intercede with God for the health of her husband. But he answered, "God wishes for him: do you desire anything but the salvation of his soul?" Both mother and sons, however, joined together entreating him to pray for Virgilio's life, and then he said plainly to them, that it was well for his soul that he should die then; and after Crescenzi's death Philip told Marcello Vitelleschi that when he really wished to pray for the deceased's recovery, he found himself deprived of the power to pray, and he seemed to hear an interior voice telling him that it was necessary for Virgilio's good that he should die then. In like manner when Antonio Regattiero went to recommend his sick wife to the Saint's prayers, Philip said, "Let her go; do not make yourself anxious about this;" and the woman died.

When Patrizio Patrizi died, his indisposition seemed so slight that he said he would get up the next morning, and the doctors declared he had no fever. Philip, however, ordered him to receive the holy communion as soon as possible, to make his will, and to prepare for death. Patrizio's wife, seeing the Saint in such a hurry, said, "This old man seems out of his mind," and Patrizio himself said, "In this matter the Father seems to me to be a little precipitate;" and yet when he had made his will and received the last sacraments he died. He was a great servant of God, and the Saint put the greatest possible confidence in him, and after his death recommended himself to his prayers.

Fra. Desiderio Consalvi, a Dominican, was dangerously ill of a pestilential fever, with lethargy and delirium; the medical men despaired of him, and he was at the point of death. At the same time and in the same convent another brother, Fra. Francesco Bencini, was in, but not so seriously as Consalvi. Philip went to see both of them; he visited Fra. Francesco first, and said, "This one will die." Going afterwards to Fra. Desiderio, he had scarcely entered his cell before the invalid came to himself, and the Saint laying his hands on his head, the delirium left him instantly, and Philip said, "Be of good cheer; you will get well." At these words the sick man felt his heart filled with joy, secretly believing that God was going to restore him his health through the means of his servant Philip; nay, he seemed to be already cured, and answered, "I trust in you, father, pray for me and for my welfare." When Philip bade him goodbye, he said to him a second time, "Keep up your heart; you will recover, without doubt." And so it was; for, contrary to the opinion of all, he recovered, and Fra. Franceso died; so that the friars, when they saw Fra. Desiderio restored to health, called him "the Risen Lazarus;" and Giovanni Comparotti, a medical man of the order, used to call this cure "the miracle of miracles." It happened on the 22nd of July, 1591.

Finally, he predicted the death of S. Charles Borromeo. Ceccolino Margarucci, a priest of San Severino, and protonotary apostolic, who had been sent by the holy father to the service of S. Charles, having asked his master's leave to stay three or four months at home, in order to settle some affairs of his own, and desiring the holy cardinal to grant him a favor before his return to Milan after settling these affairs, wrote to Philip to get him to obtain this favor for him from the cardinal. Philip replied, that it was useless treating of such matters, because by the time he thought of returning to Milan, some thing would have happened which would prevent his returning to his service there. Margarucci could not at the time understand what Philip meant; but the mystery was cleared up when he received the news of S. Charles's death, just as he was getting ready to return to Milan. He had written his letter to the holy father a month before the cardinal's death, when there was no indisposition, or anything to make men expect the sad event. When Margarucci returned to Rome, some months afterwards, Philip, as soon as he saw him, said, "Did I not tell you something would happen which would prevent your returning to the service of Cardinal Borromeo?"

Chapter 4 – Philip predicts the recovery of many

The reader must not, however, imagine that Philip was only the messenger of death. There were many instances in which he predicted the recovery of those who seemed at the point of death. Cardinal Francesco Sforza was ill of a pestilential fever and a bloody flux; and for twenty-two days the malady had afflicted him with loss of appetite and cruel pain, so that he had made his confession and received the Viaticum, but not Extreme Unction. Caterina Sforza, his mother, in this distress sent a candle to Philip, and at the same time begged him to pray for the recovery of her son the cardinal. Philip waited for a little while, and then sent word to her not to be cast down, because her son would certainly not die; and the cardinal recovered. The same thing happened to Michele Mercati, of San Miniato, a famous physician and one of Philip's most intimate friends. When he was lying at death's door, Philip said to his father Pietro Mercati, who was also a physician, "Do not be alarmed; your son will not die," and Pietro saying to him one day, "Father! we may almost count the minutes now," Philip answered, "Have I not told you that he will not die? The Lord does not want him yet: He chooses to reserve him for another time." Michele survived this eleven years, became physician to Clement VIII, and was made a prelate by him, and then Philip predicted his death, as he had before predicted his recovery. He sent several times to him to tell him not to study so hard, for that if he continued to do so he would die very shortly. Michele gave no heed to the warning, but a month and a half after he had finished the book he was composing, he died; and when the holy father heard of it, he said, "Yes, he chose to study too much."

When the second son of the duke of Acquasparta was ill, his mother sent to recommend him to the prayers of the Saint. When Philip was vested for mass, the time when they always reminded him of those who were recommended to his prayers, they called to his remembrance the request of the duchess; he answered that she had an elder son, implying that the other one would die, as he did. Shortly afterwards the elder son fell dangerously ill, and the mother sent to beg the prayers of the Saint. Philip said that he must help him by his prayers, as the other son had died but a little while before, and conformably to his prediction, and by the help of his prayers, the one who was now ill recovered. Giovan Battista Altoviti was so ill that the physician considered him as good as dead, but the Saint, having prayed for him, said to Father Francesco Maria Tarugi, "Go and tell Giovan Battista from me, that he shall not only not die, but that he shall begin to recover tomorrow, and shall get well;" all which was verified in the end.

Bartolomeo Dotti, a Modenese, was ill in Rome of fever; he made his will, and those who were about him expecting his death, watched with him through the night. He held a squire's place, and in consequence of this, his nephew begged the Saint to pray for his uncle, for if he died the place would be lost, and go out of the family, which would be a great loss to both of them; particularly as his uncle had told him several times, that he wished to resign the office in his favor. Philip answered, "Go; he will get well this time; but the first illness he shall have after this, he will die most certainly; but as to his resigning his place in your favor, I tell you he will do nothing of the kind." Dotti got well, but did not resign his place, and four years afterwards he died of the first illness which he had, after the Saint's prediction.

Olimpia del Nero, wife of Marco Antonio Vitelleschi, was dangerously ill; three fevers came one after another, and there was every symptom of inevitable death. Girolamo Cordella, who attended her, told her husband that he had never had but three patients in that way before, and that all three had died. Philip, however, told Marco Antonio and others, not to be afraid, because he felt compassion for that family, and that the loss would be too great, and that he would pray to God for her with the greatest earnestness, adding, "This is a case in which we must needs do violence to God, and pray absolutely for her, because she has so many children." The invalid began to amend as soon as the Saint had gone, and got well in a few days, contrary to the opinion of the medical men.

Cardinal Girolamo Panfilio, before he was promoted to the cardinalate, and when he was auditor of the Rota, fell sick, and every one judged his disease to be mortal. Philip went to visit him twice a-day; and once, when the malady was at its worst, moved by the spirit of God, he took the sufferer by the head, and held it tightly with both his hands. Meanwhile he trembled and was agitated in his usual way, while he prayed for him, and when he had finished his prayer, he said, "Be of good cheer, and do not be afraid; you will not die this time, but in a few days you will be free from your complaint." Panfilio began to amend immediately, and in a short time was completely well. The same cardinal affirms that this happened also to his nephew Alessandro. The physicians had already given him over, when Philip came to visit him. He did nothing but touch him with some relics, pray for him, and then say that his illness would be of no consequence. The youth's complaint took a favorable turn immediately, to the surprise of the medical attendants.

Faustina Cenci, the wife of Carlo Gabrielli, was at the point of death. The holy father went to visit her, laid his hand upon her head, and said, "Do not fear, you will not die." He then prayed for a while, and she said, "Father! I am dead." Philip replied, "No, keep up your spirits; I assure you you will not die this time;" nor was it a vain security, for in a short time she recovered perfectly. Costanza del Drago was also at the point of death, when the Saint went to visit her. He said to her, "Do not be afraid, you will soon come to confession at San Girolamo;" and so it was, for from this occasion she became one of the Saint's penitents, and confessed to him as long as she lived. Another time when Costanza was eight months gone in her pregnancy, she was attacked by a dangerous fever and measles, and her malady increased so much that she seemed at the point of death, and about midnight she received the holy Viaticum, after which the priest returned to give her Extreme Unction. Meanwhile she began to think within herself in what manner she might be rescued from impending death, and it came into her mind, that the only remedy in this urgent necessity, was Philip's intercession with the Divine clemency for her recovery. At daybreak Philip presented himself without being sent for, and found her somewhat better. As soon as she saw him she began to say, "Father! I have passed the night in distresses and fears, and have been at death's door. I longed very much to see you, because I felt sure you could assist me, and as soon as I thought of you, I implored the aid of God, and immediately through the power of your prayers I began to amend." Then Philip replied, "During this very night which you have passed in the midst of distress, I have all the while been with you; and now be of good cheer, for you will not only not die, but will soon recover your health perfectly." The lady immediately found herself better, and contrary to the expectation of all who knew how ill she had been, recovered her former health in a few days.

The same happened to the wife of Giovan Francesco Bucca, a Roman. She was at the very point of death; and the brothers of the Company of S. Giovanni de' Fiorentini were already warned to be ready to accompany her to the grave. Philip, however, went to visit her, and touching her with some relics, prayed for her, and then said to her husband, "Your wife will certainly not die;" and to the astonishment of all she rallied and recovered perfectly.

Giovanni Antonio Lucci, when he was upwards of sixty years old, fell from his horse as he was coming to Rome. He received a contusion on the head, and dislocated his shoulder bone, and he was so much injured that all looked upon his death as certain. In consequence of this accident a fever came on, and the physicians pronouncing him in danger, Giovanni Antonio sent for the holy father in order to confess to him. When Philip came, Lucci begged him to pray for his recovery, not that he was afraid of death, but because he had not settled his affairs as he should wish to do. Philip, hearing this, embraced him, and said, "Do not fear, you will settle your affairs as you wish, and you will have time to make your will at your leisure." At that moment he began to amend, and in a short time recovered perfectly, and survived the Saint some months. Philip said the same to Giovan Francesco Bernardi, a father of the Congregation, who had already received Extreme Unction, and yet recovered to the surprise of everybody. The Saint afterwards said to him, "My Giovan Francesco, I prayed for you in that dangerous illness, that God would be pleased to heal you if it was for your good." To Agnesina Colonna, a lady as illustrious for her piety as her birth, and who was then given over by her medical attendants, he said, "You will not die this time," and she recovered. Another time he visited Giovan Battista Crivelli, who was ill of a fever, and was just then expecting the usual accession, and he said to him, "Do not fear; the fever will not come again;" and so it proved. A priest, one of the Saint's spiritual children, had a rupture which inconvenienced him greatly, and he could find no remedy for it, although he had consulted some of the most skilful physicians and surgeons. He had recourse, however, to the prayers of Philip, and having recommended himself to him several times, the Saint always answered, "Do you not be afraid; you will be cured of it;" and in a few days it went away of itself, and nothing but a slight mark remained.

Finally, we may observe that those sick persons, whose recovery Philip predicted, got well, although the physicians had despaired of them, and those who he said would die did die, even when the physicians had no suspicion of it, and treated the malady as of no importance. Monte Zazzara declares that he had on several occasions two or three sicknesses in the house at a time, some sick of malignant fever, and other pestilential disorders, and telling everything to the Saint, as he usually did, if Philip said, "Do not be afraid; they will not die," they always got well; but if he did not say so, they died.

Chapter 5 – Other of Philip's predictions

Philip made many other predictions about different matters. Sulpizia Sirleti, the wife of Pietro Focile, whom we have already mentioned, had a daughter four years old, who was dangerously ill. She sent for the holy father, who was her confessor, and begged him with many tears to heal her daughter. The Saint replied, "Be calm, God wishes for her, let it be enough for you to have nursed her for God." But the mother, not quite resigning herself as she ought to do, Philip added, "Well, you will have a son, who will give you such trouble that it will go ill with you." At the end of about two years and a half she had a son, who his whole life long did nothing else but give continual displeasure to his father and mother. Elena Cibi, the wife of Domenico Mazzei, being in the pains of childbirth, sent for the holy father that she might make her confession. Having done this, she begged of him to hold at the font the child that was about to be born, or at least to find someone else to do so, according as he pleased; Philip answered, "There will be no need of a godfather;" and the night following Elena was confined of a dead child.

There was in the Congregation a lay brother, named Pietro Paolo de Petris. It happened that his father, who was a poor man, won five or six thousand crowns in certain wagers which were common at that time. In consequence of this he was very anxious that his son should leave the Congregation and study for the priesthood, in order that he might assist in raising the family. Pietro Paolo, in order to get rid of his father's importunities, determined by the Saint's advice to set off for Naples, and going for a blessing, Philip, changing his mind, said to him, "I do not wish you to go; and do not be alarmed, God will provide in this matter;" and three months afterwards Pietro's father lost all his money at play, and consequently gave his son no further trouble.

Olimpia del Nero, wife of Marco Antonio Vitelleschi, had seven daughters, and was extremely desirous of having a son. She had great faith in the holy father, and going to him she said, "Father, I have seven daughters;" Philip replied, "Well, do not be afraid; you will not have any more girls." She had three more children, all of whom were boys, and then, thinking her family was becoming too large, she went again to the Saint, and said, "Father, I have now three sons;" Philip answered, "Go away with you! you will have no more, neither boys nor girls," a prediction which was fulfilled in the event.

The Saint one day entered the convent of Torre di Specchi, and as four of those good mothers were going with him to one of their churches, which is now called the Old Church, he said to Porzia Capozucchi, who was one of them, "Porzia, give yourself to prayer;" she replied, "I cannot, father, because I am in office, and I have always active work to do." Another of them, Maria Maddalena Anguillara, said, "And what of me, father? I do not give myself up to prayer, and yet I have nothing to do." The Saint answered, as usual, in a joking way, "Yes, yes! you do nothing, and you shall be presidente; so give yourself to prayer now, for you will not be able to do so when you are superioress." The others, when they heard this, burst out laughing, for Maria Maddalena was then only about twenty or twenty-one; the Saint said, "Laugh away, laugh away, and yet you will say afterwards, 'Philip said it.'" When he saw that Maria Maddalena herself was laughing, he said to her, "You laugh, do you? remember, Philip has told you." From time to time several superioresses died, and at last, after the canonization of the Saint, Girolama Taschi was elected; but in 1635 she became perfectly blind, and being no longer able to attend to her duties she resigned her office, and at the new election the mothers chose Maria Maddalena Anguillara as presidente. Afterwards they remembered Philip's prophecy, which was thus fulfilled forty years after he had made it, and that contrary to all expectation, inasmuch as Girolama Taschi was young, and likely to live a long time.

The constable Marco Antonio Colonna, and Felice Orsina, his wife, were annoyed that their son Fabrizio had no heirs. Anna Borromeo, the sister of S. Charles and Fabrizio's wife, one of the Saint's penitents, was on this account particularly anxious to have a son, and she recommended herself to Philip's prayers, that he might obtain this favor for her from God. One morning Philip said to her quite suddenly, "Anna, you may rejoice, for in a short time you will have two sons; and a year afterwards she had a son, who was named Marco Antonio, and the year following another, named Filippo, after the constable's death; and she used to say, "I consider myself to have received these two sons through the intercession of Father Philip," and she used to call them his children.

Tommaso Minerbetti and Pier Antonio Morelli went to San Girolamo, by the advice of F. Francesco Benci of the Company of Jesus, to hear Philip's opinion of a resolution which they had made. Pier Antonio told him he wished to become a Benedictine monk, and Tommaso said his desire was to be a priest, but they wished for the Saint's advice. Philip rose from his chair, and with a cheerful countenance touched Pier Antonio with a stick which he had in his hand, saying to him, "You shall not be a monk;" and to Tommaso, "You shall not be a priest." And so it turned out, for Tommaso married after he had received minor orders; and Pier Antonio, though he did his best to be a monk, remained a secular priest, and died curate of Santa Fiora.

Captain Ottonello Ottonelli, of Fanano, in the territory of Modena, came to Rome on some business concerning the erection of a convent of nuns, and meeting with some difficulties, he was brought to the holy father by Germanico Fedeli, in order that Philip might take an interest in the matter, and help him with his prayers. As soon as Ottonelli arrived, the Saint turned to some priests who were present, and said to them, "This man is your brother." He then asked the captain what profession he was of; he replied, that he was a soldier. "No," said Philip, "not a soldier, but the brother of these;" and then, laying his hand on his head, he blessed him. Now Ottonelli was a married man, had several sons and daughters, and was exceedingly fond of his profession. In a very short time, however, his wife and some of his daughters died; those who survived became nuns, and he himself, in 1609, inspired by God, was ordained priest, and after some years became even a religious among the fathers of the Pious Schools, the order founded by S. Joseph Calasanctius.

In 1579 four of our fathers were sent by the Congregation to Milan upon business. One day the holy father suddenly called Francesco Maria Tarugi, and said to him, "Write immediately to our fathers at Milan, and tell them to return home as soon as possible." Tarugi answered, that it was not well to recall them, lest it should create scandal in that city, seeing they had not accomplished the business on which they were sent. Philip replied, "Make no answer; you obey me and write, and write that they are to come home immediately." The letter had scarcely arrived at Milan, when the plague broke out, although there had not been so much as a suspicion of it previously; and it was so sudden that two of the fathers had great difficulty in getting away, and passing the barrier on their return. One of those fathers, Pompeo Pateri, wished a few months before to go into Spain with a prelate who was greatly attached to the Congregation, as well to please the prelate as to facilitate the accomplishment of the business above mentioned, Milan being at that time under the government of Spain. The rest of the fathers were of opinion that he ought to go; the resolution was taken, and the packet fastened up to send to the post; but at the very time Philip said to Father Agostino Manni, "Write to Pompeo, and tell him not to go into Spain, but to stop at Milan." Two months had not passed before a person died, whose death would have entailed a very serious loss upon the Congregation, if Pompeo had not been in Milan at the time.

Pier Filippo Lazzarelli, a parish priest, was in danger of losing his benefice through the favor which his enemies had with a certain influential prelate. This drove him into such despair, that he left off saying mass and office, and determined to shoot his adversary and murder him. In this condition it happened that one of his brothers brought him one morning to our church, and as they were both kneeling before the high altar, the priest turned and saw the Saint at the confessional. Although he had never seen him before, he felt himself so drawn to him, that he was, as it were, forced to him, and threw himself at his feet without knowing what he was doing. Philip, seeing him full of thought, and not uttering a word, took hold of him by the ear, and said, "You are tempted, are you not?" He replied, "I am tempted to such a degree, father, that I am on the point of doing great evil," and he then told him all he had in his mind. Philip answered, "Go away, and do not be cast down; in a fortnight you will be freed from these troubles," and having said thus he heard his confession. When the fortnight had elapsed, the priest met his adversary, who said, "I give up to you now, and consider myself to have lost my cause, as my patron has been removed from his office." The priest then remembered the holy father's words, and gave God thanks for preserving him from that great sin.

The same thing happened to Orazio Ricci, a knight of Malta. He was in the service of Cardinal Frederick Borromeo, and he was afflicted by an important persecution set on foot against him in that court, and which involved his honor and reputation. He rose up one morning very early, in great discontent, and went into the open air, that he might in some measure give vent to the passion which affected him. In the street he met S. Philip, who asked him where he was going; he answered, "To take the air, but that if his Reverence wished anything else of him he might command him freely." Philip, who had seen in spirit all his distress, took him with him to the palace of the auditor of the Camera, who was at that time Orazio Borghese, brother of Paul V, with whom the Saint had some important business, and because it was so early he had to wait a long time. Meanwhile the Saint began reading; but the knight was more disturbed than ever, especially when he found himself shut up in a weary waiting room, when he had intended to be out in the open air, and yet he was ashamed to ask Philip's leave to go away. Just at the time when Ricci's weariness had come to such a pitch that he could not possibly stay any longer, Philip rose from his chair, and looking fixedly at him, took his hand and squeezed it, saying, "Do not be afraid; it will all come to nothing, and in the end matters will turn out well for you, and I tell you so." The knight was astonished at this, but at the same time greatly consoled, and filled with a lively hope that all would be as the Saint had prophesied. In a fortnight the cardinal dismissed from his service the man who was persecuting Ricci, and the knight rose higher than before in his master's favor, who at last put him as chamberlain in the household of Clement VIII, everything falling out to his advantage, according to the words of the holy father.

In 1580 Domenico Ridolfi, of the order of the Clerks Regular, was sent by his superiors from Naples to Cremona. When he arrived in Rome he heard of Philip, and went immediately to him, and found him at the confessional. He kissed his hand, and paid his respects to him. Philip, with a blithe countenance said to him, "Go cheerfully where holy obedience sends you, and attend to the salvation of souls; and know that in progress of time you will be made bishop, in order to labor more effectually for the salvation of others. But I warn you that in this journey you will run a great risk of your life, but by the favor of our Lord and his most holy Mother you will come safely out of the danger, yet not without great difficulty." The father set off for Cremona, and when he came to the mountains of Florence, wishing to pass a fosse which was full of liquid chalk, and which he did not know of, he fell in, together with his horse, and it was so deep that both the beast and himself were up to the neck. They who were in company with him were unable to assist him, and so they began to make the commendation of his soul. At that moment the good father thought of Philip, and called him to his aid. Immediately he began to have the use of his hands, and by little and little he got out of the chalk, although half dead; and the horse was afterwards extricated by the help of two pair of oxen. He arrived at Cremona, and worked for his order till 1619, when Paul V appointed him bishop of Oria; the whole of Philip's prediction being thus punctually fulfilled.

To a certain person who wished to convert all the bad women in Rome, he predicted that he would not only not succeed, but would be perverted himself, and then in the end would marry; all which happened as he had said. Indeed, those in the house observed that all he said, however casually he might seem to say it, turned out true, and this not only during his lifetime, but of things which happened after his death. For what he said, or even in any manner insinuated, was verified by degrees, and they who were in the way of knowing of them, had almost daily experience of something or other proving true which he had predicted.

Fra. Niccolo Ridolfi, a Florentine noble, took the Dominican habit when he was quite a youth, and it was the prior's will that Philip should clothe him, he did so, and he then said to him, "I make a friar of you now, and you shall one day make a friar of me." When Ridolfi was made Master General of the Dominicans, one of the first things he did, was to order the office of S. Philip to be recited throughout the whole of the order, as is done with the saints who were children of the order; and it was then men came to see how the Saint's prediction was fulfilled. Another time Philip said to Father Pietro Consolini, as if he was joking, "You will one day see me dragged through the Banchi." Many years after his death a marble statue of the Saint was made for the new sacristy, where it is at present to be seen; and although they would naturally have brought it through the Strada di Panico, yet some hindrances arose which compelled them to bring it through the Banchi. Father Pietro happened unawares to meet the kind of truck on which they were dragging the statue, and being told it was the statue of Philip, he began to weep with emotion, remembering the strange prediction, and now seeing it fulfilled.

While they were building the church of Madonna dei Lumi, at San Severino for our Congregation, the Saint said to some Barnabite fathers, "I am building for you," and so it proved in the end; for although the Congregation was established there, our people gave up the church to the Barnabites six years after the Saint's death. He also told the same fathers that they would one day have the college of S. Paul in Rome, thus determining the place of their establishment years beforehand by the spirit of prophecy. Lastly, he told the Venerable Giovanni Leonardi, founder of the Clerks Regular of the Mother of God, and one of his penitents, that he would not live to see his congregation formally and canonically erected into a religious institute, saying, "God does not choose to do everything in your time."

Chapter 6 – He prophesies to several that they will be cardinals or popes

He prophesied to many that they would be cardinals, and to others that they would be popes. Some youths were one day in his room, and among them were Pietro Aldobrandini, the Abate Crescenzi, and Marcello Vitelleschi. The holy father, without there being a vacancy in the holy see, or anything to suggest the conversation, called Pietro Aldobrandini to him, and commanded him by holy obedience, to say to his companions, "Father Philip says I am to tell you that in a short time you will have to call me Illustrissimo, and that you will esteem it as a favor to have an opportunity of speaking with me." Pietro obeyed out of the respect which he had for the Saint, but he blushed and was not a little ashamed. In a short time the holy see became vacant, and Cardinal Ippolito Aldobrandini, his uncle, was made pope, and Pietro was made a cardinal. A little while before, Philip, as if he were making game of him, said to him who was still a youth, "See how I behave to you now, whom I shall shortly have to call Illustrissimo."

Giovan Francesco Aldobrandini, nephew of Clement VIII, and general of the Holy Church, being in Philip's room, saw stuck up there two cardinal's armorial bearings, sketched on paper, with two death's heads in the shield. Wishing to know the meaning of this, he asked what those two cardinal's hats and death's heads signified. Philip, after some little reluctance, said to him, "They signify that after my death I shall have two cardinals in my Congregation;" and so, the year after the Saint's death, Francesco Maria Tarugi, and Cesare Baronius, both priests of the Congregation, were made cardinals. Philip had several times put a cardinal's berretta on Baronius's head, as if in presage of what was to happen, and twenty years before the promotion of these two priests, he had spoken of it to Mgr. Paolo Recuperati. At other times he spoke of it to others, and particularly to Francesco Neri, a priest of the Company of Jesus, who asked the Saint if Baronius would ever be pope. Philip answered expressly that he would not; so that when Baronius was in conclave after the death of Clement VIII, and was commonly reported to be near to the popedom, Francesco confidently asserted that he would not be chosen, because the blessed Philip had told him it would not be so.

Girolamo Panfilio says that Philip prophesied to him that he should be a cardinal. "When I went to confession one morning," says Girolamo, "to the blessed father, who was ill, he said to me, 'Would you like to be a cardinal?' I answered, that I had never thought of such a thing. He rejoined, 'However, you will be a cardinal.' I laughed at him, and said, 'And pray who will make me one?' however, the blessed father repeated twice over, 'I tell you you will be a cardinal.'" He received the hat from Clement VIII many years after the Saint's death.

Cardinal Innocenzo del Bufalo speaks as follows: "In 1593 or 1594, if I remember rightly, the blessed Father Philip telling me that I should have a canonry at S. Peter's, I laughed at this, because I was not in the pope's service, nor known to him, so far as I could tell, and I did not see how my appointment to this canonry could come about; and the oftener Father Philip affirmed it the less I believed it. However, in 1549, about the month of August, if I remember rightly, Cardinal Aldobrandini, without my having sought favor, or made any efforts for it, sent for me and told me that the pope thought of giving me the canonry at S. Peter's, vacant by the death of Mgr. Maffei. The following day, or a few days afterwards, I went to see the blessed Father Philip, and showed great signs of joy, which I really felt, about my appointment to this canonry; he said that this was nothing, for that this pope would also make me cardinal. This seemed so unlikely, and indeed so impossible, that I laughed immoderately at him; but for all that he repeated it several times, and on different occasions. Afterwards, when by the grace of God and his holiness I was created cardinal, I learnt that the blessed Father Philip had predicted it several times to Sister Silvia del Bufalo, my sister, a nun at Torre di Specchi; and on one occasion, when the news came to Rome of a dangerous illness with which I had been seized in France, my sister said I should certainly not die, because I must be a cardinal first, according to the prediction of the blessed Father Philip."

Cardinal Francesco Diatristano in like manner says, "When I was young, and living at Rome as chamberlain of honor to Clement VIII, Cardinal Pietro Aldobrandini took me to the church of Santa Maria in the Vallicella, to visit Father Philip Neri. We went to his room, and as soon as the holy old man saw me he went into another room, and took out of a basket a very old cardinal's berretta, and laughing at me he put it on my head, and said, "O what a fine young cardinal!" Little thinking that he had the light of prophecy, but imagining that he was making game of me, I was somewhat out of temper; but partly shame and partly respect for his age and the presence of others made me keep it down. However, not long after the event approved the Saint's action, and at the same time condemned my vexation, which I also condemn now; and I have related this matter just as it happened, for the glory of the Saint, and I subscribe it with my own hand, and seal it with my seal, in token of its truth."

As to the papacy, whenever the holy see was vacant he seemed to hear a voice telling him which of the cardinals would be pope. After the death of Pius IV four or five days before the election of the pope, Philip was with Marcello Ferro, one of his spiritual children, and lifting his eyes to heaven, and going almost into an ecstasy, he said, "The pope will be elected on Monday." Then another day afterwards, as Marcello was walking with him, he begged him, as he had already told him the day of the pope's election, to tell him who would be pope. Philip answered, "Come now, I will tell you: the pope will be one whom you have never thought of, and whom no one has spoken of as likely, and that is Cardinal Alessandrino, and he will be elected on Monday evening without fail." This was the glorious S. Pius V whose election the Saint had already predicted to others, and which took place as he had said. After the death of S. Pius V, Marcello remembered how Philip had prophesied his election, and accordingly prayed him very importunately to tell him who would be pope now. Philip asked him who was talked of in Rome as likely; Marcello answered, "Cardinal Morone." "No," replied Philip, "it will not be Morone, but Boncompagni," who was elected accordingly, and took the name of Gregory XIII.

After the death of Sixtus V, Cardinal Niccolò Sfondrato came one day to visit the holy father. Philip sent him word not to come up stairs, but to stay in the guest-room, and he would come down to him. When he came down he found there Pietro Paolo Crescenzi, who was afterwards cardinal, and Abate Giacomo his brother, Marcello Vitelleschi, and others; and before he spoke to the cardinal he commanded all of them to kiss the feet of his Eminence, which they did. A day or two afterwards the same cardinal came into our church, and Francesco della Molara went and told the Saint of it. Philip answered, "That pope, eh?" Even while Sixtus V was alive, Philip had in different ways pointed to Cardinal Sfondrato as the future pope; and once in particular, about a year before the death of Sixtus. The cardinal was in Philip's room, according to his custom, with Marcello Vitelleschi and others. Philip said to Marcello, "Open that cupboard, and give me the pope's cap that is there;" this was a cap which had belonged to S. Pius V and was preserved by the holy father as a relic. Philip took it and tried to put it on the cardinal's head, saying to him, "Try it a little, and see how well it suits you," meaning by that to insinuate what was to be hereafter. Urban VII who was chosen to succeed Sixtus, only lived twelve days, and then Cardinal Sfondrato was elected, and took the name of Gregory XIV.

But his prediction of the papacy to Cardinal Ippolito Aldobrandino, was even yet more wonderful. For some time before, the cardinal was in the garden of Curzio de' Massimi, together with Cardinal Cusano, the Saint, and some others; and Father Curzio coming to Philip, said to him, "I wish your Reverence would get me taken into the service of Cardinal Aldobrandino." Philip replied, "I will do so without fail; leave it to me; for I tell you he will not die cardinal;" and four months afterwards he was elected pope. The very evening before the election, he said to the Abate Marco Antonio Maffa, among others, that Aldobrandino would be pope, and would take the name of Clement, which he did; and that same evening Mgr. Papia sent the Saint a sonnet, asking him to pray that they might have a good pope and a speedy election, upon which Philip sent him another sonnet in reply, containing the same prophecy of Aldobrandino's election.

To Leo XI, before he was cardinal, and when he was the Grand Duke's ambassador, Philip made three prophecies in the few following words, "Signor Alessandro, you will be cardinal and pope, but your reign will last a short time." Fra. Girolamo Ghetti, a Roman, who was afterwards general of the order of the hermits of S. Augustine, when he was preaching on the octave of the Saint's canonization, declared that he heard this from Leo's own mouth when he was cardinal; and it was confirmed by Gregory XV, for when he heard what Fra. Girolamo had said in his sermon, he added, "I am sure it is true, for when I was auditor of the Rota, and went to kiss the feet of Leo XI, among other things he said, 'I shall not weary the people long, for I shall soon be out of the way,'" which was fulfilled by his early death.

Although Philip almost always foresaw who would be pope, yet he never mentioned it except for some grave reason, or in familiar conversations with some of his penitents, as if he were in joke; and he used always to add, that we ought by no means to give easy credence to similar predictions, or to wish for them, because many deceits and snares of the devil might be hidden in them; and he was very harsh towards those who went to tell him that they had had revelations or made prophecies.

Chapter 7 – Philip sees things which happen at a distance

Philip had also received the gift of seeing things absent as though they were present. Late one Sunday morning, Cesare Baronius went to confess to him as usual. The holy father would not hear him, but bade him go to Santo Spirito to visit the sick. Baronius replied that it was past the time; the Saint however replied, "Go and perform the obedience." He went, and as he was walking through the hospital, he saw a patient with the crucifix and lamp at his bed, as is usual with the dying. It so happened that the sufferer had come into the hospital the day before after the customary time, and therefore had been put to bed without having made his confession, and as he had worsened very much, they had given him Extreme Unction. Baronius went up to him, and asking him some questions, found that he had not been to confession. He heard his confession at once and gave him Communion, and the poor fellow died immediately. Baronius returned to the house and told the Saint, who said, "Well now, another time you will have learned to obey without making any answer."

Francesco Maria Tarugi went to him one morning to confession, and Philip said to him, "How is such a person? How long is it since you have seen her? go and visit her, and then come back to confession, for my heart is disturbed about her soul." This person was a servant in the hospital of San Giacomo of the Incurables, a very diligent and devout woman. Tarugi went, and found her with the cross at her bed-head, and just expiring; and he was thus enabled to assist her in this extremity. The same thing happened to a captain who was one of Philip's penitents. One morning the Saint suddenly sent some person to inquire after him, and he was found at the point of death, and was thus furnished with all that he had need of in his last hour. Costanzo Tassone had fallen into a lethargy from which he could not be roused: the Saint said to one of the fathers of the congregation, "Go to Costanzo who is dying." He went and found him asleep, whereupon he said to him, "Awake, and take the

Sacraments." Costanzo immediately awoke, made his confession, received the Communion and Extreme Unction, and then died.

As Antonio Fantini was one day going to Chiesa Nuova, someone through some slight pique threw a bucket of water on his head from a window, as he was passing through the street. This disturbed him exceedingly and filled him with resentment. When he entered the church he went to the holy father to confess; and the Saint, before he heard him, told him what had happened to him in the street, and bantered him about it, to Antonio's astonishment, who was sure Philip could not have learned it from anyone else, because no one had been a witness of it, and if anyone had been, the time was too short for him to have told it to Philip, who detailed every minutest circumstance. Upon another occasion he went out with several of his penitents, among whom was Marcello Ferro. When they came to the Campo di Fiore, the Saint called Marcello and said to him, "Who are those people whom you have at your house?" he replied, "They are gentlemen, and are so and so," naming their names. "Well," said the Saint, "I tell you that you must anyhow look to this matter, and find some remedy for it, for they are there to do mischief; and if the matter is not remedied very shortly, bloodshed will ensue, and you will find out that all I am now telling you is true." All this he said, covering his face with his hands, and in a kind of ecstasy or abstraction of mind. Marcello was thunderstruck at these words, and in the greatest possible distress. As soon as he reached home he began to pray, and begged of God most earnestly to give him some proof of what Philip had said. He then put himself upon his guard, and paid the most minute attention to everything those persons did, and soon received positive proof of what had been told him, and was enabled by a little dexterity to ward off the danger.

Paolo Ricuperati, referendary of both the Segnature, had conversed one evening with a beneficiary of S. Peter's about some secret affairs of their own. The next morning he went to S. Girolamo della Carità, and Philip repeated to him with the utmost exactness all the conversation with its circumstances, just as they had really occurred. The prelate was overcome with astonishment, because he knew that the beneficiary was not acquainted with the Saint, and perhaps did not even know him; yet in order to be quite sure, he went to him and asked him, if he had been talking to any one of the business which they had conversed upon the evening before; and when he said that he had not, Ricuperati discovered that Philip had heard and seen in spirit all that had passed between them.

On one occasion the Saint had sent one of his spiritual children to some distance, and when he returned he gave Philip an account of all that had happened since he had been away. The Saint replied to it, "I knew all this before," and yet the occurrences were such as he could not have known, except by Divine revelation. In like manner when he was once talking with Cardinal Frederic Borromeo about a secret business, and the cardinal asked him how he had come to the knowledge of it, Philip answered, "I sometimes say things, and I do not know why I say them, but God makes me speak." Muzio Achillei, a priest at San Severino, when he had returned from Rome to his own country, gave himself up to a belief in dreams and visions, and to seek after sensible sweetnesses in devotion. He never conferred with anyone about this, neither did he write a word of it to the holy father, but Philip nevertheless sent him letters warning him that he must not walk by that path, because it was easy to be deceived by the devil in those matters, and also to injure our bodily health; and furthermore he admonished him of a certain occasion of sin into which he had fallen rather by imprudence than out of an evil will, and gave him rules for avoiding similar dangers. Of all this Muzio himself affirmed that the holy father could know nothing except by Divine revelation, for he had not disclosed it to anyone.

Giovan Battista Lamberti, also one of Philip's penitents, was informed by his father that his uncle at Messina was dead. This uncle had always said that he would make him his heir, and his property amounted to more than forty thousand crowns. When Lamberti heard this, he went to confer with Philip, to make his confession, and to ask his permission to set off for Messina. Philip, laying hold of him by his ear, made him lean his head against his breast, and held him in this position for some little time. Meanwhile Giovan Battista smelled so sweet a fragrance that he had never smelled anything like it; and Philip, lifting the penitent's head up, looked fixedly at him with a joyous countenance, and said, "My son, do not disturb yourself; there is no occasion for you to leave Rome, for your uncle is now quite well, and you will shortly have a letter from him, congratulating you on your coming to court, and sending you something (naming what it was) as a proof of his affection." Lamberti had such faith in Philip that he did not set off on his journey, and the following Tuesday he had a letter from his uncle, in which he informed him of his recovery, and also sent him a present. Giovan Battista was exceedingly astonished, and went immediately to tell the news to the Saint, and to thank him. But Philip, looking rather sternly at him, commanded him never to mention the matter to anyone so long as he lived.

Giovanni Atrina of Marsico in the kingdom of Naples, one of the Saint's penitents, heard from his cousin that his mother was dead. As he was poor, he could afford to have only one mass said for her, and after that he went to Philip to recommend her to his prayers, but wept so bitterly that he could not articulate a single word. The Saint said to him, "Go your way; there is no truth in the matter; your mother is not even ill;" and a few days afterwards Giovanni heard from his mother who was in perfect health.

Giulio Severa, a brother of the Congregation, went one morning to confess to him; and as he was going, some letters were given him which contained the news of his mother's death, although he had not before so much as heard that she was ill. Without mentioning it to anyone he went to the Saint and knelt down; but before he could speak a word, Philip took his berretta off, and put it on Giulio's head, and then twined round his neck a rosary which he had in his hand, and said to him, "My son, sorrow no more, for your mother is gone to salvation; be cheerful therefore, and rejoice because of it." When Giulio heard these words he was overwhelmed with astonishment, as he had not spoken to anyone on the subject, and had only just received the news himself. But as he believed implicitly the good news which Philip gave him, he ceased to mourn, and was delighted to think that he had some one now in Paradise to pray for him.

Before concluding this chapter it will not be foreign to my purpose to relate a piece of pleasantry similar to that which S. Gregory tells of S. Benedict in his Dialogues, about the servant whose master sent him to the Saint with two bottles of wine, but he hid one by the way, and the Saint saw him in spirit, and reproved him with dexterous charity, as S. Gregory relates at some length. Marcello Vitelleschi, out of affection to Philip, sent him two flasks of orange-flower water; the servant who was carrying them inadvertently broke one of them by the way. When he arrived with the one bottle, Philip smiled, and said, "Come now, tell me the truth; you have drunk half of it on the road, have you not?" The servant hearing this, and perceiving that Philip was alluding to the non-appearance of the other bottle, told him what had happened. When he returned home, he asked his master if he had told Father Philip that he was going to send him the two bottles of orange-flower water, and learning that Vitelleschi had never said anything to him about it, he perceived that the Saint had seen in spirit the accident he had had by the way.

Philip one day sent Egidio Calvelli, a most exemplary brother of the Congregation, upon a particular business. Egidio, turning a little out of his road, took that opportunity of visiting two churches to which he had a particular devotion. Philip saw the whole of this in spirit, and when the brother returned, he asked him where he had been. Egidio, not wishing to discover the little pious act which he had done, only replied that he had been to execute the business which his Reverence had entrusted to him. The Saint added, "and where else have you been?" and he, persisting in his equivocal answer, answered, "I have been where your

Reverence sent me." Then Philip replied, "Ah you captain of gypsies! and why won't you tell me that you have been to such and such a church, in such and such a way?" mentioning all the circumstances, and leaving Egidio lost in wonder.

Chapter 8 – His knowledge of the secrets of the heart

In the way of knowledge of the secrets of the heart, Philip had such a gift of penetrating the interior of his penitents, that he knew whether they had made their prayer, and for how long they had prayed. Nay, he was generally aware of the sins they had committed, and read the thoughts that were passing through their minds. This was so well known as an established truth, that they whose consciences reproved them of sin seemed while in his presence to be actually in the fire, whereas they who had clean consciences thought themselves in Paradise so long as they were with him. Many of his penitents who were aware that the Saint perceived in spirit their actions and their thoughts, if they were together and had entered into any conversation which gave rise to a scruple of its sinfulness, would immediately stop and say, "No, no; we must take care, for Father Philip will find us out." Indeed, he himself often took occasion to say that he could tell for certain, by merely looking them in the face, if his penitents were dealing truthfully with him, or playing the hypocrite; although as a veil and out of humility, he pretended that it was merely his skill in physiognomy.

Rafaello Lupi, a Roman youth of most irregular life, was one day brought by a friend to hear the sermons at San Girolamo. When the oratory was finished, his friend, wishing to draw him into the spiritual life, took him to the holy father's room, telling Philip that he had brought him a young man who wished to make a practice of coming to the sermons, but desired first of all to make a good confession. When Rafaello heard this, he was extremely indignant with his friend, as he had no such intentions, but rather the contrary. However, not openly to affront him, he knelt down and made a false confession. Philip, aware of this, took hold of his head and pressed it strongly to him in his usual way, saying, "The Holy Spirit has revealed to me that there is not a word of truth in all you have said." When the penitent heard these words, he was moved to compunction. Philip exhorted him to make a good confession, and Rafaello felt such an instantaneous change come over him, that he made a general confession of his whole life, and from that time forward took Philip for his confessor, and by his advice became a friar of the Strict Observance of S. Francis, where he lived and died, faithful to the spirit of that holy religion.

Maria Maddalena Anguillara, an oblate at Torre di Specchi and one of his penitents, going to confession to him one day, the servant of God looked at her, and said, "Give yourself more time for reflection." She immediately retired, and examining her conscience over again, she remembered some sins which she had forgotten before, and then went once more to the holy father. At the end of her confession, full of wonder she said to him, "Father, since you can see my conscience, tell me if there is anything else." Philip in reply told her to quiet herself, for that there was nothing else. She then began to entertain a doubt whether Philip had done this by chance, or whether he had really a knowledge of her sins. But the matter was soon set at rest, for when she went to confession upon another occasion, the Saint, although she had never told him what passed in her mind, said to her, "Hold your peace, and I will speak to you;" and he then began declaring to her one by one, all the very sins which she was come to confess. Thus he not only perceived but also cured the temptation of his penitent, who from that time forward honored him as a prophet, and called him by that name.

A Roman noble, whose name I shall conceal out of respect, affirms that the Saint repeatedly manifested to him his own secret thoughts; and on one occasion when he was in doubt whether he had not some hidden sin which he had never confessed, or through ignorance had made no scruple of at the time, he begged of the Saint to help him with his prayers. Philip replied, "Do not disturb yourself, and do not doubt but that if you should not know, or if you should forget anything of consequence, God would reveal it to me: of this you may rest assured." The like happened to another Roman noble, Francesco della Molara, who, having made a general confession to the Saint, went to confession to him again afterwards; Philip said to him, "Tell me, my son, have you not committed such and such a sin?" "Yes," answered the penitent. "Why then did you not confess it?" replied Philip. "Because," rejoined Francesco, "I thought I had accused myself of it on previous occasions." "But I can tell you," added the Saint, "that you have never mentioned it in confession at all." The penitent reflected upon this, and remembered that he really never had confessed it, and he praised God for having warned him of it by means of his servant Philip.

When the cavaliere Guiseppo Zorla, who has been already mentioned, went to confession at San Girolamo della Carità, Philip not only told him all his secret thoughts in times past, but also thoughts that would come upon him hereafter, and gave advice as to the remedies he should use for each. Things came to pass just as Philip had predicted, so that he used to say that the Saint knew his heart better than he did himself. One of the Saint's penitents, in confessing to him, forgot a mortal sin of hatred, and when the confession was over and he was expecting absolution, Philip said to him, "Have you not desired the death of someone?" He said he had, and the Saint, knowing him to be otherwise in good dispositions, gave him absolution without saying anything further.

In 1591 Teo Guerra of Siena, a man of eminent virtues and great spirituality, came to Rome on some important business for the good of souls, and was lodged by the fathers of the Congregation at Chiesa Nuova. One evening he saw the holy father in company with some prelates who had come to see him, very cheerful and laughing as the others did; whereupon it came into his head that he was not a Saint as men commonly thought, else he would not be guilty of such levity, which appeared very unsuitable and unbecoming in him. The next morning he went to confess to Philip, and said nothing of the scandal he had taken the evening before. Philip, however, had perceived it all in spirit, and said to him, "Be careful, Teo, to keep perfect sincerity always in your confessions, and take this as a counsel - never out of human respect to conceal any sin from your confessor, however trivial it may be or may appear to you. Why now did you not confess that you were scandalized at me yesterday evening?" And he then told him all that had passed through his mind just in the order in which it had actually come before him. Teo, perceiving that the servant of God knew even his most hidden thoughts, conceived from that hour a still higher opinion of his sanctity, which was still more augmented when the Saint told him that he knew when anyone was under temptation.

Once during a severe famine, a poor woman went to confession to him at San Girolamo della Carità, not from any good motive, but because bread was given away there as usual, and she hoped that Philip would order them to give her bread as well as the other poor women. She knelt down therefore, and said she wished to go to confession; but Philip saw in spirit the real object for which she had come, and said to her, "In God's name, go away, my good woman, there is no bread for you," and nothing could induce him to hear her confession. Indeed the Saint stood very much on his guard against persons who were likely out of interest to outrage the sacrament of penance; and although he was full of loving-kindness, yet he was very anxious that penitents should not go to confession in order to get alms; and when he suspected that, and yet knew that they were really in need, he used to give money to other persons, and dexterously contrive that they should help such penitents without their so much as dreaming that the relief really came to them through their confessor; and thus they were not exposed to the temptation of trying to appear devout so as to gain credit with their confessor.

Philip repeatedly told his penitents when through shame they had omitted in confession any grievous fall or temptation. One day Ettore Modio in confessing to him omitted to mention the temptation of impure thoughts; the Saint however said to him, "You have such and such temptations, and you are negligent in banishing them, and what is worse, you do not accuse yourself of them," and he thus cured him of his fault. Another of his penitents, whose name I shall not mention, was assailed during the night by grievous temptations, and in the morning he was ashamed to appear before Philip, because perhaps he had not combated them as he ought to have done. He did not therefore come to confession that morning, but after dinner he went to the oratory, and although he put himself in a place where he thought be should not be perceived, he could not for all that hide himself from the holy father who saw him, and calling him to him, said to him, "What! my good man, you are trying to fly from me, are you?" And then taking him aside, he reproved him, and detailed minutely to him all his temptation, which bred no less compunction than wonder in the mind of his penitent. To the same person he once revealed a most secret matter for the good of his soul, a matter which none but the penitent himself and God could have known.

Another young man omitted out of shame to mention some grave sins in confession; and at last Philip said to him, "My son, you have not come here in sincerity, you have omitted such and such sins," naming them to him one by one, and distinguishing all the circumstances, of which, as the youth affirmed, he could not possibly have any knowledge except by Divine revelation. Whereupon, acknowledging his fault, he was filled with compunction and burst into tears, and then made a general confession to the immense profit of his soul. Another person, who had committed a most grievous sin, went to confession to him; but when he wished to begin and to accuse himself of the sin, he began to tremble and could not articulate a single word. The Saint asked him why he did not speak; "Because," replied the penitent, "I am ashamed to mention a sin I have committed." The Saint, taking compassion on his misery, took him by the hand and said, "Do not be afraid, I will tell you your sin," and he then related it just as it had happened; and the penitent, when he had received absolution, went away in great contentment, and at the same time astonished to have found a man who could thus clearly see his secret sins. The same happened in the case of another of his penitents, who out of shame had gone to confess one of his sins elsewhere, and then returned to confess the rest to Philip. The holy father said to him, "My son, you have committed a sin which you do not want me to know, and so you have gone to confess it elsewhere, but meanwhile God has revealed it to me." At these words the penitent was smitten with compunction, disclosed the whole truth, and made a good confession. To another, who had also gone elsewhere to confession, and was making some excuses for it, the Saint replied, "The fact is, you do not come here because of the great sins you have committed." Another he called aside, and said very charitably to him, "Tell me, my son, why do you not confess such a sin?" But in fact the instances are almost innumerable, in which he told his penitents of their secret sins and temptations, when they had not the courage to confess them.

But let us now speak of matters out of confession. A youth, named Vincenzo Berger, left his home one morning without any thought of becoming a friar; but as he was walking along the street, an inspiration came to him, impelling him to take the habit of S. Dominic. He went therefore to the Minerva to speak to Fra. Pietro Martire, the Master of Novices, who has been already mentioned, but he went merely to take counsel of him, never having spoken to him before either on this or any other matter. Fra. Pietro Martire said to him, "Go to San Girolamo to Father Philip, and tell him all you have told me, and if he says it is well, come back and I will take care to give you the consolation you wish." Vincenzo lost no time in complying with this injunction, and went with such speed that it was impossible that either Fra. Pietro Martire or anyone else should have got to San Girolamo before him. He found the holy father talking to another person close to the sacristy. As soon as he saw him, Philip said, "Wait, my young friend, I know what you want." Having then dismissed the person to whom he was talking, he went up to the youth, and pulling his hair and ears, he said to him, "I know that Fra. Pietro Martire has sent you here to see if I approve of your becoming a friar, or not. Go and tell him from me that it is an inspiration of God." Vincenzo returned immediately to Fra. Pietro Martire astonished beyond measure at what Philip had said to him; and when he got to the Minerva, he related all that had happened, and said, like the Samaritan woman of old, he had found a man who had revealed to him the thoughts of his heart. Fra. Pietro Martire smiled and made the sign of the cross on Vincenzo's forehead, saying, "I knew well to whom I was sending you, and since Father Philip approves your inspiration, you may be sure you will obtain what you wish." A few days after he received the habit of S. Dominic from the hands of Father Antonio Brancuti, the Provincial, in the presence of Philip and some other members of the Congregation. He took the name of Fra. Girolamo, and Fra. Pietro Martire often assured him that there was no understanding between Philip and himself in the matter, which confirmed him still more in his conviction, that the holy father knew of it by Divine revelation.

Domenico Scopa, a clerk regular, going to Rome to become a religious, Tarugi wished him to talk to Philip about it first. The holy father counselled him to carry out his intention, and then whispered in his ear that as to the secret difficulty that stood in the way of his coming to a decision, he was to make no account of it, because in religion it would not be of the least annoyance to him. Domenico was perfectly astonished at this, and at a loss to conceive how Philip could have divined the secret repugnance that he felt, inasmuch as he had never conferred with anyone about it; and he was still more astonished when he found the prediction, that it would prove to be no real annoyance, verified in the end. Father Biagio Betti, of the same religion, had suffered from some interior trials for more than a year, and had often prayed to be delivered from them, as well as practiced different mortifications for the same end. But neither those things nor the counsel of his confessor had availed. At last he determined to go to Philip, as he had great faith in him, and thought that by his means he should find a remedy for his troubles. When he got to Chiesa Nuova he found Philip hearing confessions, and stopped in the passage to wait for him. He had hardly taken three or four steps up and down before the Saint came to him, and without Father Biagio opening his mouth, he said to him, "I know what you want, you need not tell me, go and do what such a father (naming his confessor) will tell you, and that will suffice." The religious was greatly astonished, not having opened his mind to anyone except that very same confessor. However, both because of the promise he had made to the Saint, and the sure hope of his deliverance which he felt, he went to his confessor and conferred anew with him about these interior disturbances, and that very conference freed him entirely from all further molestation.

Luigi de Torres, archbishop of Monreale, and afterwards Cardinal of the Holy Church, while he was a youth, was conversing with the Saint, and observing that he had got on a garment which was somewhat torn, and that he was generally poorly dressed, it came into his mind to buy him a cassock, and one day he put the money aside for this purpose; but before purchasing the cassock, he went to hear the sermons at San Girolamo. When the Oratory was finished, the Saint who had foreseen what Luigi was going to do, conducted him to his room, and opening a cupboard said to him, "Now see I am in no want of clothes, and there is no need of your going to any expense for me." Luigi, who had told no one of his intention, was very much surprised; and afterwards when he was archbishop and cardinal, he used to relate the anecdote as a proof that Philip had received from God the gift of reading the secrets of the heart.

Claudio Neri, a Roman citizen, was so beset with scruples, that they hindered him from doing several good works, and especially kept him back from frequent communion. He had often half made up his mind to confer with others about this, and especially with the holy father, but he could not quite screw his courage up to the point. One day, when Philip was unwell, Claudio went to visit him, and when they had conversed together a little while, the Saint asked him what it was that he wished to speak to him about. He replied that he had nothing to speak to him about, but that he had come merely to visit him. The Saint, however, repeated several times that he would have him speak frankly and without reserve to him whatever he might wish to say; but Claudio always gave him the same answer. Philip then began relating all his trouble as of a third person; "there was once a friend of mine," said he, "who had an affliction which harassed him extremely;" and so he went on minutely and accurately describing Claudio's suffering, so that he perceived the holy father was speaking of him, and applying to himself the remedy which Philip pretended he had given his friend, he obtained perfect deliverance and consolation.

The same Claudio Neri had a daughter, named Maddalena, who desired to become a nun in a convent which did not meet with her father's approval, as he was anxious she should enter the Torre di Specchi. The Saint, who knew nothing of Claudio's thoughts except what he perceived in spirit, obtained, without being asked to do so, her admission into Torre di Specchi, according to her father's wish, where to her own satisfaction as well as her father's she entered and took the name of Sister Eufrasia. The same thing happened to Francesco de' Rustici, a Roman noble. He had been debating the whole night through, how he could arrange some business with one of his relations; at last he determined to go and confer with the holy father the next morning, without mentioning the matter to anyone else. As soon as Philip saw him he said, "I know what you want; come again in two days, and I will give you satisfaction." He then conversed with him for a short time about indifferent things, and Francesco went away without making any further allusion to the business most upon his mind. In two days he returned, and found that the Saint had already arranged everything in the most satisfactory manner, although he himself had given the matter up in despair, because he had no clear documents, and could not make out a case, although thousands of crowns were at stake; and he was overwhelmed with astonishment, both that the Saint should have thus read his secret thoughts and also adjusted matters so quickly.

Giovanni Andrea Pomio Luccatelli, theologian and priest of Bologna, very often read different scholastic authors in Philip's room; and frequently when he had read for a short time, the Saint would say to him, "My Luccatelli, while you are reading your attention is not fixed upon your book, but such and such thoughts (naming them) are passing through your mind;" and he told him them just as they had presented themselves to his imagination, leaving Giovanni Andrea more than once almost beside himself with wonder. When Costanza del Drago saw Philip coming to console her after her husband's death, she said within herself, "What an old man this father is, and yet he goes on living, while my husband, who was quite young compared to him, is dead." Philip laughed as he approached her, and said, "I that am so old am alive, and your husband who was quite young compared to me is dead - eh! is that it? Ah! But the secrets of the Lord are different." Costanza was greatly astonished to hear him repeat her thought so instantaneously, for she had hardly had time to conceive the words within herself. Upon another occasion she had resolved upon doing a certain pious work, but afterwards changed her mind. She had not mentioned the matter to anyone, but when she went to confession the Saint said to her, "Now why have you changed your mind, and not done what you intended to do?" a question which surprised Costanza not a little, seeing she had never breathed a word to any one either of her resolution or her abandonment of it.

In the monastery of S. Martha, a nun named Sister Scolastica Gazzi, went to speak to Philip at the grate, and to lay open to him a thought she had never mentioned to anyone else, which was a conviction that she should be damned. As soon as Philip saw her he said to her, "What are you doing, Scolastica, what are you doing? Paradise is yours." "Nay, father," replied the nun, "I fear the contrary will be the case; I feel as though I should be damned." "No," answered the Saint, "I tell you that Paradise is yours, and I will prove it to you: tell me, for whom did Christ die?" "For sinners," said she. "Well," said Philip, "and what are you?" "A sinner." "Then," added the Saint, "Paradise is yours, yours because you repent of your sins." This conclusion restored peace to Sister Scolastica's mind. The temptation left her and never troubled her again, but on the contrary, the words "Paradise is yours, yours," seemed always sounding in her ears. Philip also revealed to two other sisters of the same monastery, Sister Maria Vittoria, and Sister Prassede, secrets of their hearts which they had never mentioned to anyone, and which very much concerned the good of their souls; and to another one he revealed a temptation she had had while she was in the world, not to become a nun, the devil suggesting to her that she might be saved in the secular state and she had never mentioned this temptation to anyone.

Before the decrees of the Council of Trent were put in force, while Philip was living at San Girolamo, there fell into his hands a youth of about sixteen, dressed as a layman. The Saint, looking fixedly upon him, said, "Tell me the truth, are not you a priest?" The youth, very much surprised, answered that he was, for his family had forced him to be ordained in order that they might succeed to an inheritance of sixty thousand crowns. Philip, moved with compassion, made him stop at San Girolamo, found him an opportunity of being able to pursue his studies, and obtained from his relatives an allowance proportioned to his rank, and in the end sent him to his own country happy and consoled. Speaking of this youth the Saint told Francesco Maria Tarugi, that he knew him to be a priest by the splendor of the sacerdotal *character*, which shone out upon his forehead.

A certain person having returned to Rome after many years' absence, Philip said to him as soon as he saw him, "You are not what you used to be; you have lost your former spirit." He also mentioned to him other secret things which none but God could know, and the man acknowledged that it was all true. A priest from Naples came to visit him, and Philip asked him why he had left home; he replied that he had come to Rome on business. But the Saint was aware that he was not speaking the truth, and told him what he knew to be the real cause of his departure, and then said to him, "Now is it not true that you had such and such thoughts before you came away?" Another person, having gone to the Jewish synagogue out of curiosity, remained at the door about a quarter of an hour, and inasmuch as he did not think there was any sin in so doing, he did not mention it to Philip in confession. But after he had gone away, the Saint had him called back again, and asked him if he had confessed everything, and where he had been the day before. The penitent answered that he had been to the Jewish synagogue; Philip asked him why he had not confessed it, and then made him acknowledge his fault, as well as the Saint's gift of reading the secrets of the heart.

To show still more convincingly that what is here related of the Saint's gift is by no means exaggerated, but rather the contrary, it will not be beside our purpose to set forth how eminently Philip was privileged in this respect by quoting what others have said of it.

Cardinal Frederic Borromeo, speaking of Philip's detecting the secrets of a person's heart by merely looking at him, says, "Philip possessed this power to such a degree that he perceived the changes from bad to good and from good to bad, although they might have taken place in a very short time; so that when a certain person went into his presence on one occasion he said to him, 'You have a bad look;' upon which the man retired and made some acts of contrition; and Philip without in the least knowing that he had been praying, said to him when he saw him again shortly afterwards, 'Ah! since you went away you have changed your look.'" The same Cardinal Borromeo, being alone in his room one day, allowed himself to entertain certain thoughts about temporal affairs, such as are usually called castles in the air; soon afterwards he met the Saint, who told him all that had been passing through his mind, although he had not mentioned it to anyone. Another time the same Cardinal went to confer with Philip about certain anxieties and disgusts with which he was afflicted. As soon as he entered the room the Saint was the first to speak, and said to him, "Do not trouble yourself about what you have on your mind, because nothing will come of it."

Cardinal Francesco Maria Tarugi, speaking on the same subject, says, "It happened in my own case many times over, that he saw my secret sins before I had confessed them, and said to me, 'My son, you have run such a risk, or committed such a sin, and I obtained the knowledge of it in my prayer.'" Cardinal Ottavio Paravicino expresses his surprise at the same thing, and says, "With regard to a knowledge of the thoughts of those who were about him, I can say that instances of it frequently occurred in my own case, and I used to be astonished at his knowledge of what was passing through my imagination, and I have often heard the same from others." Cardinal Girolamo Panfilio says, "I was once anxious to consult the holy father about a thought which I had not only never mentioned to anyone else, but which I felt the greatest possible repugnance to mention at all, so that for several days I was unable to get my courage up to the point. One morning in the sacristy he took me by the hand, and without my having mentioned the matter to him, he said to me, 'I wish that we should do so and so,' going exactly through everything I was anxious to mention to him, to my no little astonishment. When I went to confession to him, one single look at me was enough to enable him to read all my secrets at once, and very often before I opened my lips he would be beforehand with me, and tell me all I was going to say." Cardinal Pietro Paolo Crescenzi says, "That he could read the heart and interior secrets of men. I know myself, because I have had experience of it in my own case, for he has told me things which none but I myself could have known in a natural way, and others have related to me similar things as having happened to themselves."

Francesco Neri, the Jesuit, says, "I once went into the Saint's room to tell him a secret, and when I had finished the Saint said that as soon as I entered the room he knew it all." Marcello Vitelleschi says, "Whenever I had a repugnance to mention any sin, the holy father was sure to ask me about it before I began my confession, and this happened to me several times. And at other times when I was perplexed with a multitude of scruples before confession, one kind look from him quieted my conscience, and I used to feel sure that if I had had any burden upon my conscience he would have spoken to me about it." Fabrizio de' Massimi says, "By only looking at me he was able to tell me all I had in my heart, and he seemed to read all my thoughts." Paolo Magi says, "Sometimes when I went to confession, before I had said a word, he would say to me, 'You have done such and such a thing, or committed such and such a sin,' and what he said was always true, and they were not open sins such as anyone might have known, so that I was greatly astonished." Nero de' Neri says, "He could read the consciences of persons, for he very often made me open a book and read to him just the very things which most troubled my conscience; and after I had read them he used to look smilingly at me, and say, 'What do you think of that book?' and I replied, 'Father, it speaks the truth.'" Marcello Ferro says, "Father Philip often looked at me in the face and conversed with me in the confessional when I went to make my confession, and told me all my actions and all I had done, as though he had been master of the secrets of my heart; and when he laid his hand upon my head, either in giving me absolution, or in bidding me good-bye, I felt a tremor all through my body, accompanied with a very great devotion, which seemed to fill me full of spiritual strength."

Muzio Achillei says, "I know by experience that the holy father could penetrate the secrets of the heart and the state of consciences; and I remember very well, as I have noted in one of my books, that in the year 1573, having fallen into some sins, I was ashamed to manifest them to the holy father, and did not tell them to him. But on one occasion as he was reprimanding (not in confession) an old woman for some sin or other, he said to her, 'You will go to hell;' at these words, which were said in my hearing, I showed some signs of levity and laughed; whereupon the Saint turned to me and said, 'You also will go to hell;' and this he said in my judgment to warn me of the evil state in which I then was. But I was a raw youth at the time, and did not as yet discern the sanctity of the holy father, and did not therefore give the matter the consideration it deserved, but still remained in the state of sin. Some time afterwards I went to confession to him, and he laid open clearly and distinctly the hidden sins which I was endeavoring to conceal. I then perceived my fault, and disposed myself to make a real and sincere confession, and thus confound the devil. Besides this I discovered that the Saint knew everything which happened to me, however secret it might be, both temptations and perils of sin, and other things, and that he knew the character of the persons with whom I associated, though he did not know them by sight."

Marco Antonio Vitelleschi says, "I went several times to the holy father, and he mentioned things to me which none but God and myself could know, and seeing that I perceived this he changed the conversation; and when I went to him with any defect, I was all fear and trembling lest he should discover it, but when I did not feel myself in any fault, I seemed to be in Paradise so long as I was in his company." Angelo Vittori of Bagnarea says, "Sometimes when I went to the holy father to ask him to pray to God for me, he would tell me that I should abstain from such and such things, specifying defects of which he was well aware, although he could not have learned them from me or from any one else, for they were secret things, and I did not go to confession to him; and whatever the Saint predicted always happened to me." Pietro Focile says, "S. Philip told me many of my secret thoughts, and very often disclosed to me some of my sins and imperfections, and particularly some disobediences of which I was guilty towards him; and he used to mention these things to me the instant I came into his presence, and before I had begun to confess, and they were things which none but God and myself could know; indeed, very often they were things which only existed in my heart, and Philip could not have learnt them otherwise than by Divine revelation."

Cassandra Raidi says, "I reckoned Father Philip to be a Saint, because the first time I went to San Girolamo to confess to him, before I had said a word to him, he told me all my thoughts, and whatever was in my mind and he could not have done this if he had not been a Saint. He used also to tell me what prayers I had said, and why I had said them." Antonina de Pecorillis says, "Two years before the holy father died, while we were talking together, he disclosed to me some of my thoughts which I had never mentioned to him, nor told even in confidence to anyone. Seeing my heart thus laid open before him, I was overwhelmed with astonishment, and said within myself, 'He could not know this except by Divine revelation;' for they were secrets of my heart, and I have never mentioned this to anyone, nor published it till now." Lastly, not to fatigue the reader, I may say that the whole of the Process is full of this truth, there not being one person who was intimate with Philip who does not affirm that he knew the secrets of his heart; so that in this more than in any other gift, more even than in that of prophecy, we may truly say of him, *Non est inventus similis illi* (There is none like him).

Chapter 9 – Of the prudence and gift of counsel which Philip had, and of many advices which he gave to guide a soul in its actions

We have already remarked on Philip's anxiety to make the world regard him as a man of little sense. But however industrious were the artifices which he practiced in order to attain this end, all were fruitless. He was known and esteemed as a man of the greatest enlightenment, not only in spiritual wisdom, but in this world's business; and his prudence and gift of counsel caused him to be resorted to as an oracle by men of every rank and condition, and even the Popes set a great value on his judgment.

Gregory XIV sent often to have his advice in matters of the gravest importance. Clement VIII made an equally frequent use of his counsel, and particularly in the re-benediction of Henry IV King of France, Cardinal Gondi, the duke of Nevers, and other great lords coming to consult with the Saint on that momentous affair. Leo XI when he was cardinal went to him several times in the week, and remained four or five hours at a time in his room, partly because of the comfort he felt in conversing with him, and partly to confer with him about important business; and when his courtiers came to accompany him home at the evening Ave, he used to say how sorry he was to leave, and how much too quickly the day had passed. This cardinal had in the court the reputation of possessing consummate prudence, and among the praises he bestows on the holy father in his deposition, he specially gives him the epithet of *prudent*; and other cardinals also did the same.

St. Charles Borromeo used to stay many hours at a time with him, not only to converse on spiritual matters, but to consult with him about the government of his church. After the death of his uncle, Pius IV, S. Charles gave his sister Anna Borromeo into Philip's care to direct her as he judged best for her soul, respecting her election of a state of life. In like manner Cardinal Frederic Borromeo ruled himself in everything after the suggestions of the holy father, and never swerved from following his counsels. By his persuasion he remained his first years in Rome, then he renounced an abbacy which he possessed, and finally consented with much reluctance to undertake the church of Milan, where he was a most zealous pastor, taking Philip's counsels for his guide in government, and receiving from his lips most prudent rules and admonitions about almost everything.

Claudio Acquaviva, the fifth general of the Jesuits, himself a man of the greatest prudence, when he went to see the Saint, used to remain with him three or four hours at a time. The superiors and leading persons in religious orders went also to seek his counsel; and Teo of Siena, speaking of Philip's prudence, says, "I have been intimate with many persons, and with religious of different orders, but I never found any one who gave such mature, holy, and prudent counsel as Philip did." It is also very much to be remarked that he generally seemed to give his answers almost at random, and yet for all that they were well-founded and highly judicious, as men plainly perceived by the result.

He was also extremely circumspect, and went to work in a matter with the greatest possible caution; so much so that although his natural disposition led him to be most ready and active in obliging others, he never went farther than was convenient, or committed himself. Thus a person of quality one day begged him to make use of his influence with the Pope in an important business. Philip replied that he could get others to speak to his Holiness about that matter, and that his interference was unnecessary, and that he did not wish thus to deprive himself of the power of benefiting those who had no one else to help them.

As to the gift of *counsel*, which some confound with that of the *discernment of spirits*, he was so enlightened that he knew perfectly well what was best suited for each one who consulted him, and he adopted in every case the means best suited for directing and advancing them in the service of God. Thus it happened that all those who by his counsel embraced the religious life (and the number of them was very great indeed) persevered in it; and on the contrary, those who embraced it contrary to his opinion lost their vocations in the end. The same was also observed in the Congregation; those who were received with his cordial assent and satisfaction have persevered to the great advantage of their own souls and those of others, whereas the few to whose reception the Saint had a certain amount of aversion have ended by deserting us; and in like manner those whom he counselled to remain in the world have been happy and successful there.

An instance of this was seen in the case of that servant of God, Giovan Battista of Foligno, a man well known for his goodness, and who passed to a better life on the 25th of September, 1621, aged eighty-three. He had a great desire to know what his vocation was, and in what state of life it would please the Divine Majesty to employ him according to his holy will. The fame of Philip's sanctity was at that time widely spread, and in the beginning of the Holy Year, the Jubilee of 1575, Giovan Battista had recourse to him, and put himself into his hands, as he was accustomed to say, like a dead man, to do just what he liked with him. First of all he went to him to repeat his general confession; as soon as he knelt down at the Saint's feet and began to read what he had written, Philip took the paper out of his hand and tore it in pieces. Giovan Battista shrugged his shoulders at this, but left himself entirely in his hands to be turned which way he pleased. Philip kept giving him various and continual mortifications, but Giovan Battista went on praying, and asking God to show him his will about the state of life which he should embrace. One day, however, when he was in the church of San Bonaventura under Monte Cavallo, which at that time belonged to the Capuchins, he heard an interior voice which said to him, "Go to Foligno, Giovan Battista, go to Foligno." He was generally in the habit of consulting Philip about everything that passed within him, but he did not at once mention this voice to him, lest he should make the Saint suspect that it was his own wish to return to his country. But the same Spirit who had spoken inwardly to Giovan Battista, prompted Philip to give him the same advice; and one day he said openly to him, "I command you to return to Foligno, for that is your vocation." In going there, however, he ordered him to hold himself in readiness to leave it at the first intimation of Philip's will, both to give him an opportunity of meriting more, and also to keep him detached from the affection which a man ordinarily feels towards his native place. There Giovanni Battista remained perseveringly to extreme old age, and to what a height of goodness he attained may be conceived from the fact, that, even while he was alive, he went commonly among all classes of people by the name of the Blessed Giovan Battista of Foligno.

Cesare Baronius is another example of Philip's gift of counsel. He repeatedly asked Philip's leave to become a Capuchin; but the holy father would never consent, and persisted in his refusal in such a way that many were scandalized at it, and thought Philip was keeping men from entering religion. Whereas he kept himself to the simple consideration, that to be a Capuchin was not Baronius's vocation, and that God wished to make use of him in a different state of life, and every one knows how the result has justified Philip's counsel. In the same way he would never allow his penitent S. Camillus of Lellis to become a Capuchin, and told him that he was not made for that religion, nor that religion for him, and that if he entered it he would not persevere in it; and so it was, for he twice took the Capuchin habit and then abandoned it, Philip all the while repeating to him that do what he would he would never be a Capuchin. He also advised Francesco Pucci of Palestrina to stay in his own country; for when Francesco went to consult Philip about his becoming a Capuchin, the Saint said, "You are not good for that religion; stay, stay at Palestrina; you will bring forth more fruit there." Francesco however could not keep quietly to this advice, so Philip at last said to him, "Well, since you wish to go, go, but you will not stay." While he was on the road to Viterbo to take the habit, there happened to him by the way some grave accident, which so moved the Capuchin fathers who were with him that they exhorted him to turn back. As soon as he came to Rome he started again for Palestrina, where he had a long and dangerous illness. This set him thinking, and a scruple rose in his mind about his having turned back again, and he thought his illness was possibly a judgment on him for this; whereupon he made a vow that if he got well he would most certainly become a Capuchin. Upon his recovery he returned to Rome, and told the Saint of the vow he had made. Philip answered, "God forgive you! Did I not tell you that the religious life would not suit you, and that you were to stay at Palestrina?" and he even wished him to procure a papal dispensation from his vow. But Francesco could by no means acquiesce in the idea of a dispensation; the Saint therefore, to remove all scruples from his mind, spoke to the general of the Capuchins about him, and then sent Francesco to him. "Well," said the general, "what is this you say? have you made a vow to enter among us?" "Yes, father," replied Francesco. "Well," rejoined the general, "you may have made a vow to enter our order, but we have made no vow to receive you. Go your way, and God bless you; we do not want you here." Thus Francesco's mind was set at rest, and he was completely satisfied, and he afterwards said that the Saint had been guided by the Spirit of God in the matter; for he became archpriest of Palestrina and brought innumerable persons into the way of the Lord, not only among the lower orders, but people of title and influence, to the great profit and edification of all.

Giovanni Battista Crescenzi, a Roman noble, was sent by his relatives to consult the Saint. Philip told him he was by no means to become a religious, he told him many things about the religious life, put before him with great minuteness the obligations of a good religious, and ended by saying resolutely to him, "This is not your vocation, and the devil keeps you in this thought in order to disturb you and your family;" and a little afterwards he added, "Nay, I tell you that you will not only not become a religious, but that you will marry:" and so it came to pass. The notion of becoming a religious went out of his head, and he married, as the Saint had predicted.

In resolving persons' doubts about the choice of a state of life, and in giving to each one the counsel that suited him best, he was so secure of the truths of what he advised, that he often said to his own penitents, "Do so, because God wishes you to do so." Cardinal Frederic Borromeo, having repeatedly heard this, said, "This is a way of speaking which few or hardly any one else could make use of." At other times Philip would say, "You will persevere, and you (pointing to another) will not;" and so it invariably happened in the end. But notwithstanding all this, when he saw that anyone would have a difficulty in receiving his counsel, or be backward to acquiesce in what he said, he left him in his liberty, and said nothing, or at least refrained from pressing his advice any longer. A youth, who was afterwards raised to high ecclesiastical dignities, asked the Saint's opinion about his idea of entering the prelacy, and Philip several times advised him not to do so. The young man however persisted in his resolution, and would by no means be turned from it. He afterwards asked the Saint if he thought he had done well; Philip answered, "I give my opinion once or twice, and then I leave everyone to do as they please; *dimitto eos in desideria cordis eorum.*" Circumstances showed afterwards that Philip was right; for the prelate died, and his dignities were the cause of the greater depression of his family after his death.

Two of the holy father's spiritual children, one whose name was Francesco, and the other Giovan Battista Saraceni, whom we have mentioned before under his religious name of Fra. Pietro Martire, were both of them struck at the same time with a desire to leave the world and take the Dominican habit. Philip at once said, "Giovan Battista will become a religious and will persevere to the end; but Francesco will give way to temptations and leave the order before the year is out;" and the prediction was verified.

Before Father Flaminio Ricci entered the Congregation he was auditor to the Cardinal of Sermoneta; and while he was conversing with God in prayer at his most serious times and when he was most recollected, he twice heard within himself a voice which he did not know, and which said to him, "Veni, sequere me." It was not long, however, before he understood the force and signification of that voice for one day he was, according to his custom, riding through the streets of Rome, when he unexpectedly met Philip, whom he did not at all know. The holy father immediately fixed his eyes upon Flaminio, and said to him with the energy and authority which God inspired into him at the time, "Veni, sequere me." At these brief but potent words Flaminio at once surrendered himself without reply or reasoning, and without interposing the slightest delay he offered at once to follow the Saint, who assented to it, and received him into the Congregation, where he lived a most holy life.

The fathers of the Congregation wished to receive into the house a youth of most excellent talents, and of whom the highest expectations had been formed as well from his devotion as from his literary acquirements. The Saint by no means relished this, but as he was a man who rather condescended to others than used his authority over them, and who preferred letting others find things out by experience rather than that they should acquiesce merely in his words, he allowed him to be received, although he said openly that the youth's reception did not please him, because he was sure he would not persevere. Not many months elapsed before the young man left without any reason at all. Thus the Barnabite fathers generally consulted the Saint before they received novices into their order, and according as he said, "Accept these, reject those," they ruled themselves according to his determination, indeed they had such a veneration for the great light which God had given him, that they allowed the provost of their new college of S. Barnabas, plenary powers in the admission of novices, provided he attended to the discreet and holy counsel of Father Philip.

Philip had two penitents, the one an Italian, the other a Frenchman, both of whom gave themselves equally up to the spiritual life, but there was more show of devotion about the Italian. One day the holy father said all on a sudden, "This Italian who seems so devout will not last, he will become a man of the world, and this Frenchman, who does not seem so fervent, will persevere to the end;" and the result verified his prediction. There was a person among the Saint's acquaintance, who gave the greatest possible edification, and on one occasion when some persons were praising him as an extremely virtuous person, Philip said, "You do not know him, he is a diabolical spirit " and so it proved, for after a few years he fell into heresy, which however he ultimately abjured. Another time it happened that a well dressed youth went to hear the sermons at San Girolamo della Carità, not to get good out of them, but to make game of those who preached, and to turn away those who frequented the Oratory. One day when he was making more noise than ever, the brothers of the Oratory, unable to bear with him any longer, had recourse to the Saint, and begged him to take some measures to prevent the annoyance. Philip answered with his usual smile, "Let him alone; he will be better than you." Shortly afterwards he was converted and became a religious, where he lived in the spirit of strict observance and died a holy death.

Among the Saint's penitents was a young Portuguese, seventeen years old, who was in the family of the Cardinal of Monte Juleiano. He had attained to such a height in the spiritual life, and spoke so well of the things of God, that the most learned men were astonished at him. He wished to embrace the religious life; and Philip, who was far from approving this project, was at last overcome by the youth's importunity, and gave him the desired permission. When the day came, on which he was to take the habit, Philip was present with Francesco Maria Tarugi and some others. While the young man was being clothed with the usual ceremonies, Philip retired to some little distance, and wept most bitterly. Francesco Maria asked him why he wept so immoderately; Philip answered, "I weep for the virtues of this my son." Tarugi did not at the time understand the force of these words; but he was not left long in the dark, for although the young friar did not throw off his habit and apostatize, he abandoned his strictness and devotion, and gave himself up to a very licentious life, to the scandal of all those who had known him in the world.

The gift which Philip had in this respect was so well known, that when Pope Gregory XIII wished to fathom the spirit of the youthful Sister Orsola Benincasa, who was just come from Naples with the reputation of sanctity, he decided upon Philip as being the fittest person to try her spirit, whether it was good or evil, and to pass a judgment upon her ecstasies, which were almost continual, so much so, that when she went to speak to the Pope upon some business she went into an ecstasy three times during the same audience, without being able to utter a word. Philip undertook this charge, and tried her with different mortifications for several months, pretending to make no account of her ecstasies and raptures, and even depriving her for a long time of the holy communion. When he thought he had sufficient experience of her, he approved her spirit as good, and presented to the Pope a fitting relation of the whole case. When she left Rome, Philip gave her several rules for preserving herself from all peril in that state, and he said to several, that because she was pure and simple God drew her to perfection by that road. On her return to Naples she lived in great fear and humility, always remembering Philip's counsels, often saying that none had known her better than he did, and praising and blessing God for having given her the guidance of that holy father, by whose advice she walked in the way of God with much humility. She passed to a better life in 1618, on the 16th of January, in the odor of sanctity.

A priest, an excellent servant of God, received wonderful and unusual lights while he was at prayer; and fearing lest he should become the victim of some delusion, he spoke to several spiritual persons on the subject, but could not find anyone to give him satisfaction, or to point out where the delusion might be. At last he addressed himself to Philip, manifested the whole matter to him, and received the most full and perfect satisfaction.

Philip's usual method of testing the spirit of others was by mortification, because he held that where there was not great mortification, there could not be great sanctity. Fra. Alfonso, the

Capuchin, commonly called Father Lupo, a man of great holiness and a famous preacher, was once in retirement composing his sermon, when the holy father, inwardly moved by God, went to find him out, and when he had discovered him, he put on a severe countenance, and speaking as "one who had authority," he said to him, "O you perhaps are that Fra. Lupo, that famous preacher, who from the applause he gets in the world fancies himself to be something greater than he is, and struts about like a peacock, showing himself off in the first pulpits of Christendom? Don't you suppose now that there are plenty of preachers in Italy wiser and holier than you?" and he continued in this strain of bitter and biting sarcasm, till those who were present were amazed and confounded at his language. Father Lupo, with his usual humility and mortification, immediately threw himself on the ground, and said with much feeling and an abundance of tears, "O Messer Filippo! you do indeed tell me the truth." Then the Saint, resuming his usual serene look and gaiety, embraced him and kissed him, saying, "O my father, go on and prosper; preach the Gospel of Christ to the people as you do now, and pray to God for me;" and he went away without another word, knowing well what he had gained for himself in that interview, as well as the gain which F. Lupo had made out of it.

Another time he went to visit a servant of God, named Sister Antonia, who was blind of both eyes. She passed in Rome for a Saint, and was confined to her bed through infirmity. When Philip went to her, he tried her spirit as usual by mortification; and this in different ways, and both by deeds and words. But nothing could disturb her heart, or in the least interfere with her perfect resignation. When the Saint had finished with his mortifications, he desired before he went away, to discover to those present the light with which God had illuminated the soul of His servant, as if in compensation for her bodily blindness. Now there was a Florentine priest there whom no one in the company knew except Philip himself. The holy father took him by the ear, and made him kneel down before Sister Antonia, saying, "Sister Antonia, let us pray to God for this poor fellow;" Antonia stretched out her hand, and took the hand of the priest and kissed it, saying, "This man is a priest, and has said mass this morning, and it is rather my business to recommend myself heartily to his prayers." Philip then departed without saying a word more, and when his disciples asked him what he thought of Sister Antonia's spirit, he said it pleased him greatly, particularly her light-heartedness amidst all the wants and infirmities which she had to endure; and she on her part used to say to all those who came to ask counsel of her, "Go to Father Philip; he is a man full of the Holy Ghost."

Fra. Filippo, a layman of the Third Order of S. Francis, and who from his works of mercy and his austere life was commonly considered as a Saint, was sent to Philip by Cardinal Agostino Cusano, the Protector of the Order, that the holy father might examine his spirit. Fra. Filippo accordingly went to the Saint, who looked sternly at him, and said contemptuously, "Who is this fellow?" he then ordered a box to be brought, containing some very small coins, and told him to take as many as he pleased. Fra. Filippo pretended to be all eagerness, as if he were going to take a handful, and after all took only one. This pleased the Saint, who however went on with his mortifications. "Ah to be sure," said he, "this fellow is more likely to be in want of bread than of halfpennies; bring him some bread." When the good brother saw the bread, he seized it with greater greediness than he had done the money, and took a mouthful of it in Philip's presence, with the air of a man who could endure his hunger no longer, and then immediately put it into his sack. The Saint then asked him what kind of a life he led, and what sort of prayer he practiced; the brother answered by knocking his teeth, his hands, and his feet together, saying, he knew no other method of prayer but that. This answer delighted the Saint beyond measure; he pretended however to be displeased, and to make no account of him, and finally drove him away. When Fra. Filippo had gone, the Saint said, "Of a truth this old man has got the spirit of mortification." He also remarked to those who were present, that so far the good man had walked in the right path, but that he was in a dangerous position, and that for his part he did not at all relish the idea of his going about in this free and vagabond way.

He said the same to Fra. Filippo himself when he came to him on another occasion, telling him that the safest thing for him was to enter regularly into the Order and put himself under holy obedience; he advised him at any rate to choose a confessor and keep always to him, allowing himself to be governed blindly by him in all things. The Saint always considered this good Tertiary as a man of great purity and simplicity of life, because whenever he came to visit him, he found him always ready and firm in receiving mortifications.

He laid down many rules for the guidance and direction of souls. First of all, he would have confessors remember that it was not necessary to lead their penitents along the same road by which they themselves had been led; as the director often finds sweetness and devotion in exercises and meditations which would ruin the health of his penitents, if he endeavored to lead them that way. He would not, however, have directors make a rule of preventing their penitents doing whatever they wished or asked, or check them too much, but he added that it was a most useful thing to make them interrupt sometimes even their own ordinary devotions, as well to recreate them as to mortify them if they should be obstinately and unduly attached to their own pious practices. He was anxious moreover that, as a general rule, penitents should make a difficulty of changing their confessors, and that confessors should not over-easily receive the penitents of others, some peculiar cases always excepted: so that when a penitent who had a confessor elsewhere came to him, he generally remanded him to his own director, and did not at all relish his leaving his former confessor in order to confess to himself. Thus Nero del Nero, whom he loved most tenderly, used to go to confession at Santa Maria in Via to Father Damiano, a Servite, and so long as that father remained there Philip would never receive Nero as his own penitent; and he taught his subjects always to follow his example in this respect.

Speaking of this very subject, Pellegrino Altebollo, priest and Canon of S. Mark's at Rome, says, "On account of the reputation which the

Blessed Philip had, and because he was commonly reputed to be a Saint, I desired to be intimate with him. So when Father Giovan Francesco Bordino, then my confessor, and now Archbishop of Avignon, went into Poland with Cardinal Ippolito Aldobrandino, afterwards Clement VIII, I laid hold of the opportunity and went to confession to Father Philip, and from that time until his death I lived on terms of intimacy with him; yet I did not go to confession to him except while Father Giovan Francesco was in Poland, which was for about a year. After his return I went and knelt down before the Blessed Philip to make my confession, but he said to me, 'Have you seen your Father Giovan Francesco?' I replied that I had not; he answered, 'Well now, for the future go to your accustomed confessor;' but I, wishing to have him for my confessor, asked him twice or thrice to be so good as take me for his penitent; he replied, 'No - we must act in this way to keep peace one with another in the Church.' "

The Saint took an especial pleasure in seeing husband and wife both go to one confessor, as well for their own peace and quiet as for that of their family, at least when they acted thus of their own accord, for he knew well how important it is to have the utmost liberty and free choice in the matter of confession.

He used to recommend a particular method for the cure of a spiritual person, who, after having lived a devout life for a long time, should be so unfortunate as to fall into any considerable fault. He said there was no surer remedy than to manifest it to some virtuous person, with whom we are on terms of particular intimacy and confidential friendship, because God will reconduct us to our former state for the sake of this humility.

He said that confessors should not in the beginning allow their penitents to do whatever they pleased or asked for in the way of spiritual exercises, because by thus holding them back it was easier to keep them persevering in devotion; otherwise they would soon grow tired, and then sloth would come upon them, together with the risk of their falling away and quitting their religious exercises altogether.

He urged upon penitents not to *force* their confessor to give them leave to do something to which they felt a strong inclination; nay, in cases where they could not very easily consult their confessor, he would have them interpret his mind in the matter, and govern themselves by that, and then afterwards, in order to guarantee themselves against any serious mistake, to confer with him upon all they had done. He told them particularly never to practice the discipline and other like things without their confessor's leave; for that he who does such things at his own caprice, either ruins his health, or becomes vain-glorious, fancying that he has done some great thing, and that a man should not so attach himself to the means as to forget the end, which is charity and the love of God and the mortification of the understanding.

He was very much against penitents making vows without the advice of their spiritual father, and he was by no means easy in giving them leave to make vows, because of the great danger of their breaking them. But if they did make them, he exhorted them to do so conditionally, and gave them this formula as an example: I make a vow to have two masses said on S. Lucy's day, on the understanding that I shall be able to do so and that I shall remember it; because if I should forget it, I do not wish to oblige myself." This was prudent advice, tending to save many persons from much disquietude.

He also made a great difficulty of allowing any one to change his state, as he would ordinarily have everyone remain in the vocation wherein God called him at the first, provided he could continue in it without sin; for he said that even in the middle of a crowd a man could attend to his perfection, and that neither trade nor labor are of themselves any hindrance to the service of God. It is true, as we have before remarked, that he sent a great number of his spiritual children into religion, both men and women, and into various orders, to the Dominicans, for example, the Capuchins, the Theatines, the Jesuits, and others; nevertheless, his greatest delight and his special desire was, that men should make themselves saints in their own houses. Hence it was that he would never permit many, who lived in the court with great profit to themselves and edification to others, to leave it and go elsewhere. He used to say, "In passing from a bad state to a good one there is no need of counsel, but in passing from a good one to a better one there needs time, counsel, and prayer." Thus, in order to try if a man's inspiration to change was good, he used to keep them, not months only, but years, because, said he, not everything which is better in itself, is better to each man in particular, and although the religious state is the highest, it is not suitable for all; but where he saw fitting dispositions and marks of vocation, he was most forward in sending persons into religion, and he sent so many subjects to the Dominicans, that the friars themselves used to call him another S. Dominic. Where, however, he did not perceive these dispositions, he was very backward in giving persons leave to become monks, unless there were some urgent reason for removing them from a proximate occasion and danger of sin; in this case he thought it better that they should enter religion at once, and actually counselled them to do so.

He said that if we wished to be at peace with our neighbors, we ought never to call a person's notice to his natural defects, or be forward to correct our brothers, but to look to ourselves first. In reproving superiors we ought to endeavor to make the blame fall upon a third person, as Nathan did to David, and they will all the more readily apply it to themselves; and Philip himself in correcting the faults of his spiritual children, used to put himself forward as having the defect of the person whom he wished to correct, in such a way that he who was really culpable took the admonition to himself. Another of his advices was, that when a man had received any repulse or offence from great people or from superiors, he should not show any anger, but return to them with the same cheerful countenance as before, because they are thus easily conciliated, and put away from their minds any uneasy suspicion of the discontent they may have caused.

His advice to women was that they should stay at home, attend to the management of their families, and not willingly go out into public. One day when he was praising Martha of Spoleto, who had a great reputation for holiness, some of his people said to him, "Father, why do you praise this woman so much?" he replied, "Because she minds her spinning," alluding to that verse of Scripture, *Manum suam misit ad fortia, et digiti ejus apprehenderunt fusum.* This holy woman was extremely devoted to the Saint, and every time she came to Rome she went immediately to him and threw herself at his feet, recommending herself to his prayers, and taking the greatest pleasure in being in his presence; for she had received from God the gift of discerning the interior beauty of his soul. So that when she saw Philip she went almost into an ecstasy, contemplating the grace and supernatural beauty which she discerned in him.

It would carry me to too great a length, if I were to recount all the instances I might of his wise counsels and admonitions; I shall conclude therefore with one of too great importance to be omitted. He used to say that every man ought to stay in his own house, that is, within himself, and not go abroad, censuring and criticizing other men's actions.

Chapter 10 – Philip delivers many who are possessed by the devil

Although Philip was rather averse to exorcising persons, God had bestowed upon him that gift also, and he freed many from the possession of evil spirits. A young woman, named Caterina, was brought from the city of Aversa in the kingdom of Naples, in order that Philip might exorcise her. Although she was a girl of no education at all, she spoke Greek and Latin as if she had been at school for years; and she was endued with such a supernatural strength, that several strong men together were unable to hold her. Every time that the holy father sent for her for the exorcisms, she had a presentiment of it, saying, "Now that priest sends for me," and then she fled and hid herself in different parts of the house, and it was a matter of the utmost difficulty to get her to the church. One day, as her friends were conducting her to San Giovanni de' Fiorentini for the exorcisms, Philip, moved to compassion both for her and them, began to pray with extraordinary fervor, and in imitation of some of the Saints, to strike his breast from time to time with a discipline of brass. The devil was at once confounded and overcome, and Caterina was delivered from the malignant possession without any further exorcism. She afterwards returned to her own country, and was never molested by the evil spirits any more.

Two years before the holy father died, Lucrezia Cotta, a Roman, had suffered for eight years successively from evil spirits, in consequence of a charm which had been made against her. The possession was principally in her heart and in her eyes. The latter were very much distorted, and the sight nearly destroyed. The pain in her heart was so great, that the rector of the parish several times thought she would have died, and gave her Extreme Unction. At other times she felt her heart, as it were, wrested out of her body, and this caused such violent movements that several women did their best to hold her down, and failed; and when this was over she was left like a corpse. In consequence of this she could neither eat nor sleep, nor find repose of any sort, so that she was reduced to that degree of weakness that she could not stand or walk without receiving support from others. While she was in this miserable condition, and was one day making her confession to the Saint, he was moved to compassion by her torments, and commanded her to kneel down. She immediately obeyed, whereupon he laid one of his hands upon her heart, and the other upon her eyes, and in that attitude prayed for her. He continued his prayer for about half an hour, and when he took his hand from her heart, she was instantaneously freed from the distress and anguish she had felt there before, and never suffered from them afterwards. Not long after Lucrezia came to confession to him again, and Philip commiserating her because of the distortion of her eyes, which not only disfigured her, but made her unable to thread her needle, said to her, "Do not fear, Lucrezia, I will deliver you from the evil of your eyes as well." Sometime afterwards she came again to confession, and Philip laid his hands on her eyes, and kept them there for more than a quarter of an hour; when he took them off, she began to cry out, "Alas! father, alas! you have made me quite blind now." The Saint smiled and said, "Do not be afraid; you will not be blind." Wonderful to relate! one hour afterwards a veil seemed to drop suddenly from her eyes; she saw clearly, and the pupils of her eyes returned to their right position, and she was never troubled with any complaint in her eyes afterwards, but was able to employ herself in the very finest needlework.

One day a lady of one of the principal families of Germany was being exorcised at Santa Croce in Gerusalemme, and the holy father was present at the request of Cardinal Ottone Truchses. When the wood of the Holy Cross, together with some other relics, was shown to her, she suffered the most fearful torments, and although many thought from her gestures that the devil would depart from her, it was not so; whereupon they called upon the Saint to come to her assistance. Philip, touched with compassion for her, and moved by the prayers of the bystanders, approached her though with great reluctance, and constrained the evil spirit to tell him on what day he would depart from her. The holy father then turned to those who were there and said, "I must tell you that this lady has not been freed as yet, because of the unfaithfulness of a person who is present here, but tomorrow the devil will depart without fail;" and so it was, for on that day and in the church of Santa Maria della Rotonda, the devil departed from her, to the great joy of her relatives, who carried her back to her own country in perfect health.

One day Philip went into S. John Lateran with Pietro Vittrici, at the time they were exposing the heads of S. Peter and S. Paul to the devotion of the people. The nave was half full of people, and at the moment the sacred relics were exposed, a woman who was possessed began to utter loud cries. The Saint, moved to compassion, and knowing that she was in reality possessed by the devil, seized her by the hair, and spit in her face, saying to her, "Do you know me?"" She answered, "I should not know you in this fashion," and then fell half dead upon the ground, but delivered from the evil spirit. The Saint, seeing the people flock round, immediately went away in order to avoid observation. Indeed he had such command over the devils, that when any possessed person was unable to go to confession or communion, he would immediately and with authority forbid them to hinder her in this respect. One morning a woman came to our church dressed like a Capuchiness, together with some other country women, and none of our people knew that she was possessed. She went up to receive communion, and when the priest held the blessed Sacrament to her she would not receive It. The Saint saw this from his confessional, whereupon he rose and went up to her, and laid his hand upon her head. She was quieted immediately, and communicated in perfect peace.

The same thing happened to another person. One morning two poor old women appeared in the church, and one of them going up to a clerk of the sacristy, said to him, "Have the goodness to call the holy father who belongs to this church." The clerk answered that the father was old, and could not come downstairs; the old woman, however, begged of him to call the father, as she wished him to hear the confession of her companion, who was possessed. The clerk again replied that really the

Saint could not come; but the old woman would not be put off, and she was so importunate with him that he himself was moved to compassion, and went to call Philip, telling him that there was a poor possessed woman, whom the evil one would not allow either to confess or communicate, and that they besought him to go downstairs and hear her confession. The Saint answered, "Drive her away; what would you have me do with possessed women?" But after a little pause, moved to pity himself, he said, "Go and tell her to wait." When he arrived in the church, he went to the confessional; the possessed woman was disturbed at the very sight of him, and had to be taken to him by force; but he merely said to her, "Kneel down, my good woman," and she was calmed in an instant, and knelt quietly down and made her confession without any difficulty. He afterwards gave her the communion; and at several other times she returned to him, and confessed and communicated in his presence with the greatest tranquility.

Another time a woman, who said she was possessed, came to the Saint; he laid his hands upon her head, and said, "Go away; he will not molest you so much as before; let me see you again;" and some months passed without the evil one giving her any further annoyance. After this he returned upon her again with such vehemence that five persons could not hold her, whereupon they sent for a certain Messer Annibale who lived at Santa Cecilia. When he arrived he asked the spirit where he had been during all this interval; the devil replied that that old man had charged him not to molest the woman for that length of time.

But the devil's pride would by no means permit him to submit quietly to Philip's empire over him; and when the Saint forced him either to go out of a person or to hold his peace, the evil one always made some demonstration of spite and rage against the holy father. Father Giovanni Antonio Lucci, as we mentioned in speaking on another subject, had received a commission from the Saint to exorcise a person who was possessed, and Philip had ordered him to give the person several blows, such as are given to children when they are whipped, in contempt of the evil spirit. The devil took this scornful insult so hardly, that the night following he appeared to Philip all black and hideous, and menacing him for the insult he had put upon him, disappeared leaving a most insufferable stench in the room. Another thing which greatly provoked the devil was Philip's sending one of his spiritual children to perform the exorcism in his stead, when he himself had been sent for to do it, as the Saint by this means showed how little he thought of the devil's power. One day Philip ordered Giovan Battista Boniperti, Canon of Novara and one of his penitents, to exorcise a virgin who was possessed by an evil spirit. In the evening the priest returned home, and having occasion to mount upon a stool to fasten some nails, the stool slid from under his feet, and he was very nearly being killed. At the very same moment in which he fell, as those in her house afterwards affirmed, the devil cried out by the mouth of the possessed woman, "I thought to have murdered him."

Although God had given Philip this gift of delivering persons from the possession of the devil, yet he very seldom exercised it, and only when he was, as it were, forced to it by others; for he said that a man should not be hasty in believing that a person was really possessed, or be swayed by every little symptom they might give of being so; because natural constitution and temperament often produce similar effects, through melancholy, weakness of head, and the like; and in women also the same things happen through over-active imagination, sundry bodily infirmities, and even pretenses of possession assumed for different ends and purposes. On one occasion a girl was brought to Father Niccolò Gigli, who was, as her relations asserted, possessed, because in the night she went screaming about the house, breaking the plates, upsetting everything she could lay hands on, and committing all manner of fooleries. The case was described to the holy father, and he was asked to go and visit her; he went, and saw at once that it was all whim, whereupon he called the girl's brother and said to him, "If you wish to cure your sister, give her a sound beating whenever she begins her fooleries, and that will bring her round without any further trouble." Her brother acted upon this advice; the girl soon confessed that she had no evil spirit about her, but that it was all imposture from beginning to end. On another occasion also a girl was brought to him who was playing the part of a possessed person; when the Saint saw her he said to the relatives who brought her, "This girl is not possessed," and in the end his words were discovered to be true.

Another time a woman, named Sidera, the wife of Giovan Camillo Paloccio, was brought from Sabina to Rome, inasmuch as every one believed she was possessed. One morning when her relations had determined to take her to S. Peter's to the Pope's blessing, she went to throw herself into a well; but there being several persons near at hand, she was got out without having suffered any injury. They then took her to the blessing, and afterwards carried her several times to the Church of Spirito Santo de' Napolitani in the Strada Giulia, to have her exorcised by some priests who dwelt there. After they had bruised her all over with the blows they gave her, and almost suffocated her with continual fomentations, her friends were at last advised to take her to the holy father. As soon as he had seen her and prayed for her, he said to her friends, "She is not possessed; she is insane; have patience with her therefore, and do not put her to any further suffering." She lived a long time half silly, and breaking out from time to time into some foolery or other.

He was therefore very urgent with his subjects that they should not be credulous in this matter, and never exorcise women except publicly in church, and in the presence of seven or eight witnesses, because of the many grave dangers and suspicions which may arise out of such occurrences.

Chapter 11 – Philip while alive appears to several persons in different places

Another of the remarkable gifts which Philip had received from God was that of appearing in several places at once, particularly to assist those who recommended themselves to him in perils either of soul or body.

One of the fathers of the Congregation had, at Philip's recommendation, undertaken the charge of a beautiful boy, and he afterwards thought that this might prove an occasion of sin to him. He had never mentioned this to the Saint, or to any others who might have told him of it, but while he was in great trouble about the matter, one night when he was asleep in his room at the Vallicella, he heard the door open, although it was locked in the inside. Awakened by the noise, although he had no light in the room, he could see the holy father, who then lived at San Girolamo, entering the chamber. Philip went up to the bedside, and said to him, "How are you?" He replied, "Very ill," alluding to the affliction of his mind and the thoughts that disturbed him. Philip, laying his hand on him, made the sign of the cross, and said, "Do not fear." He then vanished, and at the same moment all the good father's trouble vanished also, and never returned to molest him again. When he got up in the morning he found the door still locked, just as if no one had been in.

Another time, one of his penitents wishing to go to Naples, consulted Philip about it. The Saint told him that he was by no means to go, for that he would either be taken by the Turks or run a risk of being drowned. The penitent, however, determined to go in spite of Philip's dissuasion; and when they got out to sea the ship was attacked by the Turks. Many of those on board threw themselves into the water, and he among the rest, but as he did not know how to swim he was on the very point of being drowned. Seeing that his death was at hand, he remembered what the holy father had said to him, and recommended himself to him with all his heart, begging him to extricate him from that danger. Wonderful to relate, Philip appeared to him instantly, and taking him by the hair, said in his usual way, "Do not be afraid;" and holding him in this manner he drew him safely to the shore.

When his old penitent, Marcello Ferro, returned from Egypt to Italy, the ship on which he had embarked was assailed by two Turkish galleys under Cyprus and captured by them. The enemy put the merchants in chains, where upon Marcello betook himself to prayer, and recommended himself most earnestly to God, beseeching Him by the merits of Father Philip his confessor to deliver him from so great a peril. At that instant he saw the holy father appear, and heard him say his usual words, "Do not be afraid; recommend yourself to God, and you will not be a slave;" and so it turned out, for when they were going to seize him and put him in chains, as they had done the rest, the captain of the Christian ship said to a renegade on board the Turkish galley, "What are you going to do with that poor old invalid? he is not good for anything." The renegade was moved to compassion by these words, and let him go. When Marcello arrived at Rome, he learned that at the very time in which he recommended himself to the Saint, Philip had said to the fathers of the Congregation, "Let us say some prayers for a certain penitent of mine who is just now in the greatest possible danger."

Costanza del Drago, a Roman lady, being very much out of humor with a person about her, would not speak to her, or humble herself to her in any way; and on this account she did not go to confession as usual, but continued in this bad temper three or four days. Early one morning when she was half awake and half asleep, she felt some one shake her so vehemently that she awoke, and heard the voice of the Saint saying, "Now how long are you going to remain in this bad humor?" Terrified by this voice, she acknowledged her fault, and went that same morning to confession to the Saint, telling him all that had happened. He made as though he knew nothing at all about it, and returned her no answer. Lucrezia Giolia, a most devout lady, wife of Giovanni Animuccia, was his penitent, and he had assigned to her fixed times of prayer, and told her to get up in the night at such an hour. She, however, often failed in this, and allowed herself to be overcome by sleep, upon which the holy father said to her, "If you do not get the better of this negligence I will come and wake you myself." And so he did, for every time she did not get up she distinctly heard the voice of the Saint calling her, "Lucrezia, get up;" and when she went to confession Philip would say, "Now did I not call you last night?" The same lady one night had a great temptation of impurity, and in the morning, without her saying a word, the Saint said to her, "You combated bravely last night, and behaved yourself as you ought to do," whereat she was overcome with astonishment to think how the Saint could have known anything about it.

On one occasion Cesaro Baronius was dangerously ill in his rooms at San Giovanni de' Fiorentini, and as he had already lost his senses all the medical attendants gave his case up as hopeless. After he had received Extreme Unction he fell asleep for a short time, and in his sleep he saw the holy father, who was at San Girolamo at the time, praying before Christ, who appeared as painters represent Him rising from the tomb, and His most holy Mother, and pleading for the health of Baronius; and he heard him say with great emotion, "Give him to me, Lord, give him to me; restore him to me; I wish for him." He persevered in this request for a long time, but Christ always appeared to deny it; at last he saw the holy father turn to the glorious Virgin, beseeching her in the most urgent manner to obtain this favor from her Son, and he perceived that at her prayers our Lord granted it. At this Baronius awoke fully persuaded that he should not die of that illness; and in fact he began to amend instantly, and to the astonishment of all he recovered perfectly in a very short time; so that he himself affirms in several places that he owed his life as well as his learning to the prayers of the holy father. When Philip went to see him, Cesare related this vision to him and thanked him, as he used to do for everything; but Philip, with his usual pious dissimulation, replied, "It is a dangerous thing to believe in dreams, so keep yourself resigned to the Will of God."

Mattia Maffei, whose dream we related before, was ill and despaired of by the physicians. The Saint went to see him, and carried with him two cases of relics; notwithstanding the decision of the medical men, he said to the invalid, "Do not be afraid, but have faith in Jesus Christ; you will not die;" and as he was going away he laid his hand upon Mattia's heart, and pressed it very strongly, giving him his blessing. About the ninth hour of the night Mattia heard Philip's voice calling him three times, and saying, "Get up," and the voice was so strong that it inspired him with fear; but rousing himself he found that he was free from fever, and in two days he left his bed perfectly recovered. Cardinal Frederic Borromeo relates that on one occasion a penitent of the holy father's was surprised at midnight by a horrible vision of a huge dog or some other beast standing at his bedside in order to attack him. He remained a long time in this distress, and when he awoke he found himself extremely dejected, and weary and sore as though he had been beaten. He went to Philip in the morning, and told him what had happened to him in the night; the Saint replied, "I can tell you that I was with you and fought for you. God sent you this vision for such and such a purpose, and it was I who prayed him to send it."

Pier Francesco Giusto, a priest and one of Philip's great friends, went from Rome to an abbey which he possessed, and remained there two years suffering from a severe and inveterate rheumatism, which had so reduced him that he could not use any of his limbs even for the most necessary purposes, and one man was unable of himself to lift him. He tried all kinds of remedies in vain, and the physicians considered his complaint incurable. At last by their advice he was put into a litter to return to Rome, but when he arrived there his complaint was so much worse that he besought God in His mercy to let him close his eyes in peace, for the pain was so acute and excessive that he fainted several times in the day. Meanwhile a priest of our Congregation visited him, and told him in Philip's name that the holy father was coming to see him and comfort him that evening. After supper the sick man was tormented by his usual pains till midnight, when Philip suddenly appeared to him and pressed his face with his hands. Pier roused himself in great fear, not knowing how the Saint could have entered, as the room door was fast, but he was not able to articulate a word. The Saint asked him how he was; and his tongue being at last loosened, the patient recommended himself most earnestly to Philip, and begged him to obtain from God the favor of his recovery. The holy father then took both his hands and put them into the shape of a cross. Pier remained thus for some time, not knowing what would come of it all; and he then heard Philip say, "Get up." At these words he rose and sat upright, a thing which he had not been able to do for many months, and he then put his legs out of bed as if he was going to get up; upon which the Saint said, "Now see, you are not so bad after all; but mind and do not say anything," and with these words he instantly disappeared, the good priest being so completely cured that he went out of doors that same week, and in a short time not a vestige of his complaint remained.

Giovanni Animuccia went upon one occasion to Prato in Tuscany, and while he was there he went to visit Sister Caterina Ricci, of the order of S. Dominic, now commonly called the Blessed Caterina of Prato, whose Life has been written by Fm. Serafino Razzi of the same order. In the course of conversation Giovanni asked her if she knew Father Philip Neri; the servant of God replied that she knew him by name but not by sight, but that she had a great desire to see him and to converse with him. In the year following Giovanni returned to Prato, and when he visited Sister Caterina again, she told him she had seen and spoken with Father Philip, although Philip had never left Rome nor Caterina Prato. When Giovanni returned to Rome, he told the Saint what had passed between Caterina Ricci and himself at Prato, and Philip confirmed all that she had said. Speaking of Caterina on the occasion of her death in 1590, in the presence of several others, Philip said openly that he had seen her while she was alive, and he described all her features one by one, although, as was said before, he had never been in Prato, nor she in Rome; and when he saw the engraving of her which was published, he said, "This picture is not like: Sister Caterina had different features."

Chapter 12 – He raises a young man to life, and command a lady to die, who was in danger of yielding to temptation if her agony endured longer

In addition to the gifts already mentioned, it pleased the Divine Majesty to confer on Philip the power of working miracles, through which he was not less wonderful in his lifetime than after his death. For both before and after his death, as we shall see, he not only restored health to the sick and delivered many from various dangers, but was even so far favored by God as to raise the dead to life. I shall content myself with relating an instance of this here, leaving the other miracles to be mentioned separately in the two last books, which will be more convenient for the reader, who can refer to them without interrupting the thread of the narrative, and can there see how eminent was the gift of miracles which Philip had received.

Fabrizio de' Massimi, who has been so often mentioned, had five daughters by his wife Lavinia de' Rustici, and she was again pregnant, and the pains of labor had even commenced when Fabrizio went to ask the holy father to pray for his wife. Philip, reflecting for a while, said, "This time your wife will have a son but I wish you to give him the name I shall choose; do you agree to this?" Fabrizio answered, "Yes." "Then," replied Philip, "I will give him the name of Paolo." This however was not the only time he had made this prediction to Fabrizio; he had said the same to him several times before. As Fabrizio was returning home he met one of his servants, who was coming to tell him that Lavinia had been delivered of a boy; and the name of Paolo was given him according to the agreement with Philip. After Lavinia's death, and when the boy was about fourteen years old, on the 10th of January, 1583, he fell sick of a fever, which lasted sixty-five days continuously. Philip went to see him every day, for he loved him tenderly, and had heard his confessions ever since he was a child. He was so pious a boy, that when Germanico

Fedeli, wondering at his patience through so long and painful a malady, asked him if he would like to change his present illness for Germanico's health, he replied that he would not barter it for the health of anybody, as he was quite contented with his sickness.

On the 16th of March the poor boy was reduced to the last extremities; and as the holy father had desired to be informed when he was on the point of expiring, they sent to say that if he wished to see him alive he must come as quickly as possible, as matters were now at the worst. The messenger arriving at San Girolamo found that Philip was saying mass, so that he could not speak to him. Meanwhile the boy expired; his father closed his eyes, and Camillo, the curate of the parish, who had given him Extreme Unction and made the commendation of his soul, was already gone; and the servants had prepared water to wash the body, and linen cloths to wrap it in. In half an hour's time the holy father arrived; Fabrizio met him at the top of the stairs, and said to him weeping, "Paolo is dead;" Philip replied, "And why did you not send to call me sooner?" "We did," rejoined Fabrizio, "but your Reverence was saying mass." Philip then entered the room where the dead body was, and throwing himself on the edge of the bed, he prayed for seven or eight minutes with the usual palpitation of his heart and trembling of his body. He then took some holy water and sprinkled the boy's face, and put a little in his mouth. After this he breathed in his face, laid his hand upon his forehead, and called him twice with a loud and sonorous voice, "Paolo, Paolo!" The youth immediately awoke as from a deep sleep, opened his eyes and said, as in reply to Philip's call, "Father!" and immediately added, "I forgot to mention a sin, so I should like to go to confession." The holy father ordered those who were round the bed to retire for a while, and putting a crucifix into Paolo's hand he heard his confession and gave him absolution. When the others returned into the room Philip began to talk with the youth about his sister and mother, who were both dead, and this conversation lasted about half an hour, the youth answering all questions with a clear distinct voice, as if he had been in perfect health. The color returned to his countenance, so that those who saw him could hardly persuade themselves that anything was the matter with him. At last the holy father asked him if he could die willingly; he replied that he could. Afterwards Philip asked him a second time if he could die willingly; he answered, "Yes, most willingly; especially that I may go and see my mother and my sister in Paradise." Philip then gave him his blessing, saying, "Go, and be blessed, and pray to God for me;" and immediately with a placid countenance and without the least movement Paolo expired in Philip's arms. During the whole of this scene Fabrizio was present with his two daughters, afterwards nuns at Santa Marta, and Violante Santacroce, his second wife, and Francesca the maid, who had attended Paolo during his illness, together with some others.

If it be a miracle to restore life to the dead, it is not less so to command a person to die and to be at once obeyed; for in both cases nothing short of the omnipotence of God is required. Philip had received from above this gift also, and like S. Peter of old, separated body and soul by a single word. The anecdote just related would be sufficient to prove this, for when the boy expressed his readiness to die, he died the instant Philip bade him; but the following instance will still more clearly establish our Saint's possession of this gift. One of the chief ladies of Rome had been ill for more than a month, and Philip went repeatedly to visit her. She was at last reduced to extremities, and when the holy father went there one day he found her in her agony, and apparently in great distress of mind. He stayed there a little while, to assist and console her in that hour of need, and then departed with the intention of returning to the Vallicella. When he had gone some way he stopped and said to those who were with him, "I feel constrained to return to that sick woman," and going back he found her in the same condition, and it seemed as though she was not going to die yet, but would continue till the following day. He went up to her, and sending away some ladies who were there, he laid his hands upon her head, breathed once or twice into her face, praying most earnestly for her, and uttering some words with the greatest emotion. He then fixed his eyes upon her, and said in a loud voice which several persons heard, "Soul! I command you in the Name of God to depart from this body;" and at the same instant the lady expired. He then told those who were present that if she had remained in her agony much longer she ran the risk of giving way to certain temptations, and that on that account he had prayed to God to accelerate her death.

Chapter 13 – Of the opinion men had of Philip's sanctity

The goodness of God in endowing Philip with so many and so great virtues and gifts rendered him an object of wonder, so that all men held him to be a Saint; and he was esteemed and revered as such by persons of all ranks of life, even by the popes themselves. Paul IV being satisfied of his holiness, as we have before related, had such an esteem for him that he not only recommended himself to his prayers, but said that he was sorry his onerous duties prevented his attending the exercises of the Oratory. Pius IV had such a veneration for him that he showed it not only during his life, but in his last hour desired to have Philip's assistance, from the value that he set upon his prayers, and he died in the Saint's arms. S. Pius V, during the disturbances about the Oratory, not only approved the exercises, but said that he was delighted to have men in Rome to rouse and quicken the devotion of others, as Philip did; and Philip on the other hand had always the very highest opinion of the sanctity of that great Pontiff, and kept by him as a relic a red velvet shoe which S. Pius had worn, and took it to the sick when he visited them. In one instance he went to pray with a lady, and afterwards touched the seat of her disease with this slipper, and she was healed. He used also to keep out of devotion a papal beretta belonging to S. Pius, as has been already mentioned before.

Gregory XIII had the highest opinion of Philip's prudence, and sought his counsel in matters of the greatest moment; and besides this he was so convinced of his sanctity that when he gave him an audience he would not allow him to stand or even to be uncovered, but made him sit, and with his cap on, conversing with him with even more familiarity and confidence than with his most intimate friends and relations; and when the Saint was with him, he would keep even his own nephews waiting, so as to have more of Philip's company. Sixtus V had such an esteem for him that he gave him with great readiness the bodies of the holy martyrs Papias and Maurus, and conferred several favors and privileges on the Congregation. Gregory XIV was not content with asking his advice in matters of importance, and making him sit covered in his presence, but revered him so much that when Philip went to kiss his foot at the beginning of his pontificate, the Pope would not allow him to do so, but came forward to meet him, and as he embraced him, said, "Ah! my father, though I am greater than you in dignity, you are greater than me in sanctity."

Clement VIII held Philip in such reverence that he recommended himself to his prayers in almost everything which befell him; and when he was ill he said several times to a friend of his, in allusion to his not getting well, "Father Philip is not praying to God for us." When Philip was unwell he often sent someone to visit him. He also desired to have him for his confessor, as he had been so before he was Pope, but Philip excused himself on the ground of his old age, and gave him Cesare Baronius in his place. When the holy father went to visit him, which he frequently did, the Pope used to go and meet him, to embrace him and kiss him, and make him sit by his side with his head covered; and when they separated they used to kiss each other; and what is still more remarkable, the Pope used often to kiss his hand with the greatest tenderness, as Gregory XIII had done before; and before Clement VIII was Pope, he seemed to think no pleasure so great as that of being in Philip's company. Before he was Cardinal, when he was Auditor of the Rota, a person went to give him some information respecting a cause in which he was concerned, and in the course of conversation he mentioned that he went to confession to Father Philip; upon which the auditor said: "That father is truly a Saint, and he will be canonized some day for certain."

As to the opinion which the cardinals had of him, we may gather it from what they themselves have written and deposed in their public testimonies. First of all, Agostino Valerio, Cardinal of Verona, wrote a little book while the Saint was alive, called *Philippus, sive de laetitia Christiana.* In this tract, among other praises which he gives him, he calls him the Christian Socrates, and shows how exactly such a name suits him. "That Christian," says he, "may truly be called Socrates, who despises all external things, is a keen enemy of every vice, cultivates virtue assiduously, is a very master of sincerity, a propagator of true discipline, perpetually teaching humility, and that not in words only, but by example, opening out the bowels of compassion to all with the most genuine charity, bearing with the infirmity of many, instructing some, assisting others by his useful counsels, commending all in his holy prayers to the Most High, and by devout exercises of this sort preserving a perpetual cheerfulness."

Cardinal Gabriello Paleotto, the first archbishop of Bologna, was one of Philip's penitents, and in the book which he wrote *De bono Senectutis*, he proposes Philip, who was still living, as the true portrait of a holy and virtuous old man, passing a most beautiful encomium upon him, and among other things saying these words: "There is no doubt but that from ancient chronicles, and particularly from the sacred histories, we could easily select many old men wonderful for their sanctity, and at the same time rich in those gifts mentioned in their proper place in this work; but inasmuch as things which we can see with our eyes and touch with our hands make a stronger impression upon us, and give more strength and luster to a truth, we have determined to use as our example a living man, and to put him forward as the exact picture of honorable old age, which any one may behold. Yes, we speak of a man who lives at this day, and whom all may see, who has lived indeed in Rome, the very theater of the world, these fifty years and more. He has spent his days so as to win the praises of all, guiding all kinds of persons along the path of Christian virtues, and animating as well as assisting them wonderfully in the service of God. This is Father Philip Neri, a Florentine, who has come to the age of eighty, and, like a mighty tree, for a long time has afforded to the people the various fruits of his virtues." On the first leaf of this book the good cardinal had a portrait of Philip, who was still alive; but before the publication of the book he was already gone to Paradise.

Cardinal Agostino Cusano had such an affection for our Saint, and revered him so much, that he was almost always in his room; and speaking of his holiness, he says, "I never knew any one, whether religious or secular, who was held in such veneration as Philip, and that by all kinds of men, as well princes as private persons. This arose from the opinion they had of his sanctity, and the evident fruit of his labors in directing souls in the way of eternal salvation. He has put an end to apparently irreconcilable dissensions of many years' standing, and which several prudent and devout men had been unable to appease, and he has done this with the greatest ease and sweetness in a very short time; and I have always esteemed his many virtues, which seemed to shine forth all the more for his trying to conceal them." Cardinal Frederic Borromeo, who as well as Cardinal Cusano went by the nickname of "Father Philip's soul," had such an opinion of his sanctity, that he speaks of him in the following terms: "During all the time that I was intimate with this venerable man, he always appeared to be so full of Divine gifts and to excel so much in virtue, that I think he might be compared with many who are spoken of with admiration by the ancient authors. He had such a science of spiritual and interior things, that we may say that he brought to bear upon himself and others, according to their various necessities, all that Cassian, Climacus, and Richard of S. Victor have written upon the subject. In a word I may conclude by saying that no one ever satisfied me so completely as Philip did, so much so that when I sometimes reflected within myself, and inquired what was wanting to his perfection, I was constrained to answer, Nothing." Indeed so great were the love and veneration which this holy cardinal had for the Saint, that he had a picture of him in wax, while he was yet alive, and carried it about him with the most reverential affection.

Cardinal Ottavio Paravicino, speaking of Philip, says as follows: "By the grace of God I first came to know Philip when I was about six years old; from which time I was allowed to enjoy his constant intimacy and familiar confidence till I was twenty-eight, when business called me into Spain; and during all that time, as well as after my return from Spain till his death, I watched minutely all his actions, movements, and words, and knew him to be a man burning with the love of God." A little after he says, "I give God infinite thanks for His kindness in giving me such a master, whose great virtues were known to all the world, and whose praise will endure for ever." This cardinal was so devoted to Philip, that it seemed as if he could not live without him, and he often spent whole days and nights with him. When the holy father was ill, it was his peculiar delight to serve him, as he did before he was cardinal and when he went once to visit him during his last illness, the Saint sent all the others out of the room, and then turning to the cardinal, said to him, "Ottavio, I wish to talk with you, but when I cough and have occasion to spit, I wish you to hold the basin and wait upon me as you used to do." The cardinal replied, "This, my father, is the greatest kindness and favor your Reverence could show me." The Saint said this to him not out of any want of proper respect for his dignity, but in order to satisfy the longing which he perceived the cardinal had to wait upon him; and the cardinal himself speaking of this, says, "I took such pleasure in serving the father, that although I sometimes suffered much from cold, hunger, and personal inconvenience, I felt a sweetness, a great sweetness in waiting upon him; and every time that I call to mind the services I did him, a joy comes over me mingled with regret that I did not serve him for a longer time." After he was cardinal he used to boast of the services he had rendered to the Saint, in making his bed, sweeping his rooms, and other like offices, particularly for the space of eight years.

It was the boast of Cardinal Ottavio Bandini, that he had served Philip's mass from a boy and speaking of his sanctity he says, "the opinion men had of his holiness was such that he was not only revered by all, but the majority went so far as to think that they could not make any progress in the spiritual life unless they put themselves under his direction; so that people generally went to the blessed Philip as they would to an oracle, to obtain from him a rule of life, and persons of every rank and condition resorted to him." A little after he says, "Whoever has been intimate with the blessed Philip, and has been a witness of his manner of living, and the pure and holy tenor of his actions for so many years, cannot doubt but that the remarkable favors obtained from God through his means while on earth, and through his invocation since his death, were real and illustrious miracles. For myself I saw them to be so numerous and so remarkable, that I always considered him to be a servant of God, and I think him now worthy to be esteemed and reverenced as a Saint for the innocence of his life, for the miracles he has wrought, and because of the common consent of men in his favor." The good cardinal used also to glory in having received a box on the ear from Philip when he was a boy; it was given him in good humor, in order to make him remember a piece of advice which the Saint gave him.

Cardinal Francesco Maria Tarugi, when he was archbishop of Avignon, wrote a letter while the Saint was living, in which he speaks as follows: "I could wish I was one of those who enjoy the first places in the little chapel where the holy father says mass, narrow though it be. But in spite of all the spacious realms which lie between me and it, by the grace of God I am continually present there in faith and love towards my dear father, as I believe that I also have a particular place in his memory, and when he opens his mind towards God in contemplation, I think that I do not sit upon the last seats. S. Catherine of Siena made herself a cell in her heart, and in that little chamber she could be alone with Jesus even when there were crowds around her; and I should wish in like manner to make myself a cell deep in my father's heart, for I believe I should find Jesus there in all the steps of that wonderful and divine life of three-and-thirty years, during which he conversed with us on earth; and when the holy father exults, and his heart leaps within him from excess of love, I would fain exult and leap with him." And towards the conclusion, he says, "As for you, enjoy this felicity so long as it pleases God to allow it you; I too might have enjoyed it for a long time, but as I did not know how to make a right use of it, I am now deprived of it through the just judgment of God upon my sins."

Cardinal Girolamo Panfilio was intimate with Philip for a long time, and he extols him greatly. "He received every one," these are the Cardinal's words, "with the greatest charity, and assisted and comforted him in such a manner that no one went away from him dissatisfied, or without considering him a man of great holiness. For my part I always regarded him as a Saint, adorned with all the virtues that we should look for in a true servant of God, and almost every day some fresh proof of his holiness was furnished by his actions up to the very day of his death." Cardinal Ludovico Madrucci was so attached to him that he repeatedly went to his room to converse with him, and he had such an affection for the institute that he often went to hear the sermons at the Oratory at San Girolamo. Cardinal Bonelli, nephew of S. Pius V, knowing the esteem his uncle had for Philip, loved him most tenderly, and revered him as a person of eminent sanctity and devotion. He often went to visit him, and desired to have Philip often with himself. Cardinal Alessandro de' Medici, archbishop of Florence, afterwards Leo XI, went to Philip at least once a week, and remained the whole day in familiar conversation with him, as it seemed as though he were in Paradise so long as he was conversing with the Saint. Cardinal Pier Donato Cesi used to show him singular respect, and for this reason conferred many benefits upon the Congregation. Cardinal Gulielmo Sirleto loved and esteemed him to such a degree that it seemed as though he was never tired of speaking of his sanctity. The same may be said of Cardinal Antonio Caraffa, and Giulio Antonio Santorio, Cardinal of Santa Severina, who was also his penitent, and always regarded him as a man of eminent and special gifts.

Besides these the following cardinals may be mentioned as having esteemed Philip as a Saint: Cardinal Alessandro Farnese, Ranuccio Farnese, Cardinal of Sant' Angelo, Girolamo Aleandro Cardinal of Ceneda, Ottonne Truchses Cardinal of Augusta, Cardinals Colonna, Gesualdo, Gambara, Savelli, Ferrerio, Salviati, Ascanio Colonna, Mondovi, Gaetano, Gondi, della Rovere, Gonzaga, Morosino, Toledo Bellarmino, Antoniani, Sfrondato, and Pepoli, all of whom were joined to Philip in the bonds of the closest intimacy.

The religious of almost all the orders loved him excessively, but none more than the Dominican fathers, to whom he sent a very great number of his penitents. Hence it was that when he went sometimes to the church of the Dominicans, or to San Silvestro on Monte Cavallo, or to Santa Maria degli Angeli, or other religious houses, those servants of God, because of the opinion they held of his sanctity, would come out to meet him and kiss his hand and beg his blessing, as if it were an angel of the Lord whom they beheld. Indeed, the most eminent and distinguished in the different orders, and not the common religious only, had this esteem for him. Father Franceschini the conventualist, a man of holy life and a famous preacher, not only went very often to him to consult him about his own affairs, but used to pay the greatest attention to the sermons at the Oratory, and used to preach there himself repeatedly. Fra. Evangelista the Observantine, surnamed Il Marcellino, a most famous preacher, and who died at Aracoeli in the odor of sanctity, had the greatest veneration for Philip. Fra. Francesco Panigarola, of the same order, Bishop of Asti, and an excellent preacher, was a great friend of the holy father, and thought so highly of his sanctity that he said to several: "Philip is a living relic." Alfonso the Capuchin, surnamed Father Lupo, used to watch Philip with the utmost reverence, and hung upon his words, and humbled himself to the ground in his presence. Fra. Paolino of Lucca, a Dominican, esteemed throughout his order for his doctrine and purity of life, submitted himself so completely to Philip's opinion, and considered him so enlightened in the things of God, that when he refused out of humility to accept one of the chief offices in his order in spite of the prayers of his brethren, as soon as the Saint bade him accept it he obeyed and accepted it without any further opposition. In a word, a very great number of religious, celebrated both for their literary acquirements and their devotion, and remarkable for their miracles as well as their virtues, revered Philip as a Saint; but for the sake of brevity we must pass them over.

The esteem and reverence which his spiritual children had for him may be gathered from what has been already narrated. While he was still living they used to take his things and keep them as relics. When his hair was cut they secretly collected it and carried it about them with reverence, as if it were a holy thing. One day the Saint perceived this and had the hair thrown out of the window; his penitents went to the place where it had been thrown and secretly collected it. Some of them also preserved small quantities of his blood, and in particular one whole bottle of what he shed from his mouth in the copious bleedings of his last illness. Others were not wanting who went to such an excess in their esteem for his sanctity, that their devotion led them, while he was still living, to say three times every day, "Sancte Philippe ora pro me," and some said it in the form of a chaplet sixty-three times every day. Some kept his portrait in their rooms among the pictures of the other Saints, and genuflected before it every morning before they left the house. Many would never allow a day to pass without going to get his blessing, and some of them kissed his feet. Others again were so anxious to remain in his company that even when they were young and their companions invited them to go to recreation with them, they would not go, and they used to be quite afraid lest the Saint should tell them to go with the rest, because their greatest recreation was to be in his company; and they used to ask him to pray that they might die before him, that they might not have to live deprived of his conversation.

They had such confidence in his prayers that they used to say, "I hope in the goodness of God, that if I shall ask anything of Him through the intercession of Father Philip, I am sure of getting it if only it be for His glory." Others said, "If I look at my life I consider myself a lost man, but through the prayers of Father Philip I hope to be saved." Some were so possessed with the idea of his being a Saint that they said, "If news was brought me that Philip had raised the dead, nay, if I had seen him do it with my own eyes, I should not be a whit surprised." Indeed, as I have heard from many and most fully believe, neither his beatification nor his canonization increased the opinion his followers had of his sanctity; for it seemed to them that they could say in the words of scripture, *manus nostrae contrectaverunt,* our own hands have handled what the holy Church and the chief Pontiff have now solemnly determined. As to the titles and praises which men gave him, it would seem almost incredible if I were to mention them all; some called him an angel, others a prophet, others Moses; some honored him with one name, others with another, but all spoke of him as of one come from heaven. There was one of his penitents who became a Capuchin friar, and when one of his friends was going to Rome the good friar exhorted him to put himself under the direction of Father Philip of Chiesa Nuova; "for," said he, "that father is an apostle, a S. Peter, a S. Paul." His friend hearing this was rather scandalized at such language, as savoring too much of exaggeration; but when he arrived in Rome and had become intimate with the Saint, he was astonished at all he saw and discovered in him, and said, "Truly that friar did not speak without reason." Father Francesco Cardone, a Dominican, who was intimate with the Saint for forty years, and greatly admired his conversation, used to pronounce this beautiful eulogium on him, *Philippus in humilitate magnus, in castitate angelus, in paupertate dives.*

Almost everyone had the same high opinion of him, and many held for certain that he had arrived at perfection in every virtue, and ruled his passions as he pleased without any difficulty; nay, he secured to have acquired dominion over the first impulses and motions of them. Gentlemen of rank, as well as his spiritual children, esteemed it a favor to be allowed to make his bed, to sweep his room, and to clean his shoes; they were rivals one to another in waiting upon him, and especially in his illnesses. They paid as much attention to his words as though they had been so many oracles. In the Process there is hardly a single witness who does not call him a Saint, and his own disciples commonly thought he deserved to be canonized, and many affirmed that it was enough to look at him to be convinced he was a Saint, for his very face breathed sanctity.

The abbot Marco Antonio Maffa had such an esteem for him, that he could not speak of him without apparently using excessive language, and mentioning his sanctity he says, "Although I am the vilest sinner in the world, yet ever since I knew Father Philip intimately I have venerated him as a Saint; and when I went to confession to him I felt him breathe sanctity into me, particularly when he gave me absolution, and I had not the same feeling when I made my confession to others; and I had also a particular devotion at his mass. In a word, cardinals, bishops, and prelates of every rank, if only they had been intimate with Philip, had an extraordinary veneration for him, and most of them kissed his hand with great devotion.

Last of all, saints themselves regarded him as a saint. S. Charles, when he came from Milan to Rome, used to go and spend four or five hours with him; and when he was at Milan he frequently wrote to him to ask his advice about different things of almost daily occurrence. He was often seen on his knees before Philip, kissing his hand and shedding floods of tears. He spoke of him to his own people as a Saint, and recommended himself to his prayers with the greatest earnestness. As he was leaving his rooms one day he said, "Philip is a man of great sanctity and of a wonderful sincerity." He took such pleasure in being with him, and had such a relish for the exercises he had instituted, that on one occasion he remained a whole day in our house. It was the Feast of S. Francis, and after saying mass, he gave communion to such crowds of people, that it occupied him from dawn till after midday. The famous Dr. Martino Navarro omitted to say mass in order that he might receive the communion from S. Charles. After this he examined minutely the institute of the Congregation, and the fabric of the church and house; he was present at the sermons during the day, and at the Oratory in the evening, and he remained to sup and sleep with us. In the morning he went away greatly edified, and said to the members of the Congregation, "O happy you who have a man to give you such laudable and holy institutes." He got Philip to preach in Sant' Ambrogio del Corso, and assisted at the sermon with the greatest attention. Philip also frequently went to hear S. Charles, as is represented in a picture in that same church; and they repeatedly said office together.

That servant of God, Fra. Felice the Capuchin, now a canonized Saint, had such a reverence for Philip that he often went to get his blessing, and knelt to receive it. One day he saw him from Monte Cavallo at a great distance, whereupon he ran and threw himself at his feet and kissed his hands. Philip embraced him closely, and they both remained for some time without uttering a word, and then parted, like S. Louis of France and Brother Giles the companion of S. Francis, who saluted each other and parted without breaking silence, having, as it were, conversed with each other inwardly. Another time S. Felix went to him at San Girolamo and knelt down as usual and asked his blessing; Philip, however, would not give it him, but knelt down himself and asked S. Felix for his blessing, and they both remained for some time on their knees in this holy contest and embracing one another. It was the common custom both of S. Felix and of Fra. Raniero, his companion and a man of great holiness, to kneel before the holy father and ask his blessing; and the pleasure they had in his company was so great that it seemed as if they could never tear themselves away. The servant of God, S. Caterina of Prato, who has been mentioned before, wrote to Philip as a Saint, and recommended herself to his prayers. His penitent, S. Camillus of Lellis, S. Ignatius Loyola, and the Blessed Alessandro Sauli, Bishop of Pavia, all reverenced him as a Saint, as may be gathered from their Lives.

The venerable Sister Orsola of Naples held him in such veneration that she speaks of him in the following manner: "By order of Pope Gregory XIII I was put under the direction of Father Philip, in whom I discerned a great love of God and a heart always on fire with that love; and when he spoke to me he seemed to tremble all over through the desire he had of drawing souls to God. As for me he was at great pains to try my spirit. At first he reviled me excessively in order to prove me, and then I knelt before him, and said that he had a true knowledge of me, and I kissed his feet. Then he said, 'Now do you make the same reproaches to me,' and he was quite importunate with me that I should revile him, from which I perceived his great humility. Also it happened that in his presence I had my usual ecstasy, which indeed is my cross; and when others called me I heard nothing, but when Philip called to me by the most holy Name of Jesus, his blessed voice penetrated me in such a manner that I returned from my ecstasy, a thing unusual with me, and discerned the power of God in him. Also upon another occasion, in the church of San Girolamo, I went into an ecstasy when I received the communion from him. When mass was finished he ordered me to walk with him, and although I was out of myself with the ecstasy, he caused me to obey and to walk with him."

The venerable Sister Francesca del Serrone of San Severino, whose Life was printed some years ago, came to Rome in the Jubilee of 1575, and after having a long conversation with the Saint, she said that Jesus was born in his heart, and that he had the spirit of S. Catherine of Sienna; and she esteemed him so much that she not only obeyed his maxims, which she considered as so many precious jewels, but she also kept as a relic a coif which she had on her head when she went to confession to him, simply because he had touched it in giving her absolution.

In fine, so universal was the opinion of Philip's sanctity, that people came to him not only from all parts of Italy, but from France, Spain, Germany, and all Christendom; and even the infidels and Jews who had ever any communication with him revered him as a holy man.

Book IV: His sicknesses and his death

Chapter 1 – Philip's last sicknesses and the apparition of our Blessed Lady

Philip, loaded with years and merits, was now drawing towards the close of his life. In the year before his death, during the month of April, he was attacked by a tertian fever, which lasted for several days; and he was scarcely recovered from this when in May he was seized with such excessive pains in his loins that in a few days his pulse was almost gone; he took next to no food, and could hardly speak so as to be understood. He passed his time however in the greatest peace; he made no complaint, and gave way to no restless movements of his limbs, but only kept saying in a low voice, "*Adauge dolorem, sed adauge patientiam*; Increase my pain, but increase my patience too." He remained in these agonies from ten to twelve hours without the pain in the least diminishing, and suffering from a retention of urine; and about three hours before the Ave Maria, the medical men, Angelo of Bagnarea and Ridolfo Silvestri, came to see him. They felt his pulse, and said that he had now but a very short time to live; they then closed the curtains and began to talk in a low voice with those who were in the room. Of these some were inmates of the house and others were strangers, but they were all spiritual children of Philip, and were all overwhelmed with grief at hearing of the approaching death of their beloved father.

They gradually became silent, and had remained so for some little time, when suddenly the Saint began to cry out with a loud voice, "He who desires any other than God deceives himself utterly, he who loves any other than God shall fall shamefully ... Ah, my Madonna, my beautiful Madonna, my blessed Madonna!" He said this with such earnestness and vehemence of spirit that he made the whole bed tremble. At hearing his voice, the medical men ran to his bed, and one of them drew the side-curtains, while the others who were in the room drew aside the curtains in front; and there they saw the holy father with his hands lifted up towards heaven, and his body raised up in the air about a foot above the bed. He kept stretching out his arms, and seemed to be embracing someone with great affection, and continued to repeat the same words, and weeping most tenderly he added, "I am not worthy, for who am I, my dear Madonna, that you should come to see me and take away my pain? and what shall I do if I get well, I who have never yet done any good?" Those who stood by were all astonished, some began to weep, others had a feeling of dread come over them, while the rest looked on attentively to see what would be the end of this sudden change. The medical men now inquired of him what the matter was, on which Philip, lying down again on his bed, answered, "Did you not see the Blessed Virgin who came to free me from my pain?" Having said these words, he seemed to return to himself, and looking round and seeing so many persons present he covered his face with the sheet and burst into tears. He remained weeping in this way for a long time, till the medical men, fearing that it might injure him seriously, besought him to stop, saying, "No more, father, no more." Then the Saint spoke to them openly and said, "I have no longer any need of your services, the Madonna has come and healed me." On this the medical men felt his pulse, and found that the fever had quite left him, and that he was cured; and the next morning he got up from his bed. Angelo da Bagnarea, as soon as he got home, wrote a minute account of all that had happened, and although Philip had earnestly besought the physicians not to tell anyone what had occurred, they were no sooner out of the house than they began to spread the news of it abroad. It soon came to the ears of the Cardinals Cusano and Borromeo, who came immediately to congratulate the holy father, as well on having recovered his health, as on having received, as they had heard, a visit from the Madonna. They were both very urgent that he should relate his vision to them, and after much entreaty, Philip, who loved them tenderly, was prevailed on to recount it to them exactly as it had happened. Cardinal Borromeo, knowing what a consolation it would be to his Holiness Clement VIII, immediately wrote an account of it and sent it him. During the whole of that evening Philip did nothing else but recommend, not only the two cardinals, but all who came into his room, to have a great devotion towards the Blessed Virgin, and he did this with the greatest earnestness and tenderness, saying, "Know, my children, and believe me who know it, that there is no way more powerful to obtain favors from God than through the prayers of the Blessed Virgin;" and he exhorted them to say frequently those words we have already mentioned, "Virgin Mary, Mother of God, pray to Jesus for me."

In the following year, 1595, he was again seized on the last day of March with a fever, which was so violent, and accompanied with such a shivering, that he was unable to speak a single word to the Cardinal of Verona, who had come to see him. This illness lasted during the whole of April. He had, however, prayed to God to let him say mass on the 1st of May in honor of Saints Philip and James, who were his especial patrons, and his prayer was heard, for on that morning he celebrated and gave communion to several of his spiritual children; and he seemed so strong and hearty that it was clear that God had miraculously cured him. He himself had foretold that he should recover, even when everyone had given up all hopes of him; for he said to Nero de' Neri, "I intend to give you communion on the Feast of Saints Philip and James, for I know that these saints will obtain for me the grace to say mass on that day, and I shall say mass then." Nevertheless, out of obedience to the medical men, who advised him to wait till his health was quite re-established, he abstained from saying mass on the three following days, though he communicated every morning as usual. At the end of that time he recommenced and celebrated daily up to the 12th of May.

On this day, which is the festival of the martyrs Nereus and Achilleus and Flavia Domitilla, the patrons of the Congregation, he was suddenly seized with so violent an effusion of blood from the mouth, that he remained without any pulse and without any hopes of life. As they feared that every moment would be his last, Cesare Baronius, who was at that the superior, not being able to give him the Viaticum, administered Extreme Unction in the presence of Cardinal Frederic Borromeo. When Philip had received this Sacrament he seemed to revive a little, whereupon the Cardinal expressed a wish to give him the Viaticum with his own hand. The instant he entered the chamber, bearing in his hand the most holy Sacrament, the holy old man opened his eyes, which till then had been closed, and with great fervor of spirit cried out with a loud voice and with many tears; "Behold my Love, behold my Love; behold Him who is all my Love and all my Good; give me my Love quickly." He said this with such affection and tenderness that it made everyone weep. When the Cardinal in giving him the Sacrament pronounced those words, *Domine non sum dignus*, Philip repeated them with such devotion and with such a loud voice, that it seemed as if nothing ailed him, saying, "No, Lord! I am not worthy, and I never was worthy, for I have never done a single good thing." In saying this he wept bitterly, and went on for some time uttering similar words; at the moment of receiving the communion, especially he cried out, "Come, Lord, come to me, come, O my Love;" then having communicated, he added, "Now I have received the true Physician of my soul; *Vanitas Vanitatum et omnia vanitas*; he who wishes for any other than Christ, knows not what he seeks nor what he wishes." During the rest of that day he remained quite quiet and comforted. In the evening he had three or four similar attacks, during which he lost a great quantity of blood, suffering at the same time extreme pain. He was not at all disturbed at this, but raising his eyes to heaven, he said, "Praised be God, who allows me in some sense to return him blood for blood." Seeing one of his spiritual children who was present looking very much alarmed, he turned to him and said, "Are you afraid? I have not the slightest fear."

It was perfectly true that he had no fear, for that which, as we have said, he so ardently desired, was now approaching. These attacks were followed by a cough, with such a difficulty in breathing that the Saint frequently exclaimed, "I feel that I am dying;" and although they administered a great many remedies, nothing was of any service to him. Notwithstanding this, when the medical men came to see him on the following morning, Philip said to them, "Your services are not wanted, my remedies are a great deal more efficacious than yours, for I sent very early this morning to give alms to several religious houses, in order that they might say masses and pray to God for me; and from that time I have not vomited any more blood, I am free from pain, I have no longer any difficulty in breathing, and I feel so much better that I seem to have perfectly recovered." The medical men felt his pulse and found that what he said was true, at which they were greatly astonished, and declared that this convalescence was nothing less than miraculous. From that day down to the 26th of May, Philip enjoyed perfect health; every day he recited his Office, said mass, heard confessions, and gave communion; so that everyone thought that he would live at least to the end of that year.

Chapter 2 – Philip foretells his death

Long before it happened, and on many occasions, Philip foretold not only his death, but the day and the hour, the manner of it, and the place where he should be buried.

First, he predicted it by saying several times in his different sicknesses that he should not die then; and God in His goodness went on discovering to him by little and little what his intentions were concerning him. In the year 1562, he was laid up with an excessive pain in his right arm, which brought on a fever, and at last reduced him to such a state that he was given over by his physicians, who were men of great reputation, namely, Ippolito Salviati, Stefano Carasio, and Bartolomeo Eustazio. Hereupon those who were attending him wished him to receive the Viaticum and Extreme Unction; but the Saint called Francesco Maria Tarugi and said to him, "I do not wish to neglect preparing for death (he had then just made his general confession), but be assured that I shall certainly not die of this sickness; for God, who of His goodness has hitherto bestowed such graces on me, would not have left me so exhausted of devotion as I am now, if this were the hour of my death." He used often to say when he was ill, that God would not let him die without first letting him know of it, and without giving him an extraordinary supply of fervor and devotion. Hence in one of his last sicknesses be said to Cesare Baronius, "Cesare, they are making great prayers for me, and yet I seem to grow no better; but on the other hand I have no feeling that I shall die;" and accordingly he recovered from that sickness. So also in the present instance, after he had received the Viaticum and Extreme Unction the fever suddenly left him, and then the pain in his arm gradually diminished; upon which he got up and returned to his ordinary employments as usual without going through any period of convalescence.

In the year 1592, about the 20th of November, he fell very ill of a fever, which lasted a long time, so that everyone thought he would certainly die of it. One evening Girolamo Cordella came to see him, and on leaving him he said with great sorrow to those in the house that the father was certainly near his end. Next morning he returned to see whether the Saint was still living, whereupon Philip called him and said, "My Cordella, believe me, I shall not die this time as you think;" and so it turned out, for on the following day he suddenly recovered and returned to his usual duties.

This sickness was so serious and lasted so long, that his subjects asked him to let them go to confession elsewhere, for Christmas Day was close at hand; the Saint, however, would not allow them, but said, "Have a little patience, I myself will hear your confessions this Christmas," and so he did.

On the last day of March in the year in which he died, he wrote to Father Flaminio Ricci Firmano, who was then at Naples, to desire him to return to Rome as soon as possible, for he wished to see him before he died. This father was very much beloved by Philip, and was the third Prefect of the Congregation after the death of the Saint. Flaminio wrote in reply, to say, that he would willingly return, but that he should be unable to do so before September; upon which Philip again desired him by all means to return immediately. He still, however, delayed, being detained by several persons of high rank, especially by the archbishop of Naples. Philip, therefore, had him again written to twice, urging him to come back, but in the second letter he said, "You will now be too late," and so it turned out. Twelve days before his death Philip said to Nero del Nero, who was congratulating him on his having recovered his health, "My Nero, I am cured, and I feel no pain whatever, but still I have but a few days to live, and my death will be when least expected, and it will take place just at the dawn," all of which actually came to pass. He knew so well that he should die suddenly, that he was always saying, "My children, we must die," and he said those words so often, that many got quite tired of hearing them, and said to him, "Father, we know very well that we must die." "That is enough," said Philip; "I tell you that we must die, and yet you do not believe it." At the time when he was ill of that spitting of blood which we have already mentioned, the abbato Marco Antonio Maffa said to him, "Never fear, father, God will make you live a long time yet, if for nothing else, at least for the good of others' souls." To which Philip replied in his usual joking way, "If you will be good enough to enable me to live to the end of this year, you shall be handsomely rewarded." Three years before his death he had promised Father Francesco Zazzara, who was then a youth of eighteen, that before he died he would instruct him in what he was to do, and what rules he was to observe after his death. The young man therefore often reminded him of this promise, and the Saint always replied, "Do not fear, I pray for you every day in my mass, and I will tell you whatever the Lord may please to reveal to me; do not think then that I shall die without first telling you what I want you to do; you have put your confidence in me, and therefore I do not intend that you shall be disappointed." So that although Philip was several times in danger of death, he never said a word to Francesco till the ninth day before he died, when he suddenly called for him and told him all that he had so long promised to tell him; upon which the youth began to weep, believing that the Saint would now very shortly die, and he was not mistaken. Ten days before his death, Philip called one of the brothers, named Giovan Battista Guerra, and asked him, "What day of the month is this?" He answered, "The fifteenth." "Fifteen," said Philip, "fifteen and ten make twenty-five, and then I shall go."

A few days before he died, he made them collect all his writings, letters, and memoranda, and had them all burnt; he had never done anything of this kind in all his other sicknesses, and therefore every one considered it a sign that his death was now fast approaching. So also he used often at this time to say to Father Germanico, "I have given you a great deal of trouble, but I shall not do so much longer." One evening he took his hand and pressing it said, "O Germanico, what things I shall see ere many days are past!" He repeated this several times, so that Germanico began to grow frightened, thinking that some dreadful disaster was about to befall Christendom; but after the death of Philip, he understood what the Saint meant by those words.

On the 18th of May the same Father Germanico having to go to Carbognano, a place about a day's journey from Rome, where the Congregation had some property, he came to the Saint for his blessing, and said, "I do not like to leave Rome, unless your Reverence will promise me that on my return I shall find you alive and well." Philip inquired, "How long shall you be away?" To which he answered, "I shall certainly return by the day before the Feast of Corpus Domini." The Saint remained silent for some time, after which he said, "Go, and come back by the time you mention." He therefore started for Carbognano, and having remained there some days, on the night before the Vigil of Corpus Domini he had a dream, in which he seemed to be in the room of the holy father at Rome, whom he saw ill in bed, and he heard Philip say to him, "Germanico, I am dying;" to which he answered, "Father, you have often been in greater danger and God has spared you to us, and He will doubtless do the same now;" to which the Saint replied, "I am going this time." At this moment he awoke, and fearing that Philip might really be dying he resolved by all means to set out at once for Rome, notwithstanding the earnest entreaties of the people of Carbognano that he would remain with them over the festival. He started therefore very early in the morning, and immediately on his arrival went to the Saint, whom he found alive and well, he kissed his hand, and Philip said to him, "You have done right in returning; it would have been a mistake had you remained longer:" and the following night Philip died.

On the day before the Feast of Corpus Domini he sent for Father Pietro Consolino to his room; and making him put his hand upon his breast and touch his ribs, which were broken and pushed outwards as we have described, he said to him, "Remember that you say mass for me." Father Consolino replied that he had already done so, and that he always said mass for his Reverence when he had no other obligation; "but," added he, "I was not aware that you were in want of it now, for you have quite recovered." "The mass," said the Saint, "that I ask of you is not the mass that you are speaking of, but the Mass of the Dead." On the same day a woman named Bernardina, who was about eighty years of age, lay dying, and was apparently so near her end that the attendants began to prepare the water for washing the body after death, for in fact she was in her agony. The sub-curate of the parish, Father Antonio Carli, on taking his leave of her told her that he would go and recommend her to the prayers of Father Philip, which he accordingly did. Philip therefore began to pray for her, and shortly said to him, "Go, Bernardina shall recover, and I shall die." At the very instant that Philip began to pray for her the sick woman broke out into a sweat and soon recovered, and on the night following Philip died.

He also predicted the place where he should be buried; for one day, a short time before death, when he was talking with Father Francesco Bozzio, he said to him, "Francesco, I mean to come and take up my abode near you;" to which he replied that the room was not a suitable one for his Reverence; but Philip repeated that he was quite determined to take up his abode near him; and so in the end it turned out, for when Philip died, his body was deposited in a little chapel above the arches over the church opposite the organ on the Epistle side, which little chapel was close to the room of Father Francesco. The same day on which he died, that is, on the morning of the Feast of Corpus Christi, after having heard the confession of Francesco della Molara, he asked him about his income, what state his affairs were in, and made a number of other minute inquiries, telling him at the same time what he ought to do as well in his temporal as in his spiritual affairs, a thing which he had never done before during the whole time that Francesco had gone to confess to him. He afterwards said, "Francesco, remember that for the future you always come to the Oratory to hear the sermons, and do not forget to read spiritual books, especially the Lives of the Saints;" he then embraced him with unusual tenderness.

Giovan Battista Guerra, whom we have spoken of before, was the warden of the church; and he one day said to Philip, "We have arranged the place where the fathers and brothers of the Congregation are to be buried." To which the Saint replied, "Have you prepared a place for me?" "Yes, Father," said Guerra, we have prepared it just under the high altar, on the epistle side." "But you will not leave me there," said Philip. "Yes, we shall, Father," said the other, "we shall leave you there." "No," said Philip, "you will put me there, but you will not leave me there." Guerra was silent; but the event proved the truth of Philip's words, for after his death he was placed by order of Giovan Battista in the place that had been prepared for him under the high altar; but on the following day, by orders of the Cardinal of Florence and of Cardinal Borromeo, the same Giovan Battista removed the body of the Saint from that place to the little chapel we have just described.

Chapter 3 – Philip dies in peace on the night after the Feast of Corpus Domini, on May 26, 1595

As the time drew near when the Saint was to depart from this life, he said mass every morning with such wonderful joy and fervor, that it was evident he knew his time was short. The Feast of Corpus Christi having at length arrived (it was a festival for which he had a particular devotion) Philip gave orders very early to admit all who wanted to come to him to confession; he began very early in the morning hearing the confessions of his spiritual children, just as if he was in perfect health. He begged many of them to say a rosary for him after his death, assigning it to some as their penance; to others he gave many spiritual instructions, particularly enjoining on them the frequentation of the Sacraments, the attending sermons and reading the Lives of the Saints; he also embraced them with great affection, and caressed them in an unusual manner. The confessions being ended, he recited the Canonical Hours with extraordinary devotion, and then said mass in his little chapel two hours earlier than his usual time. At the beginning of his mass he remained for some time looking fixedly at the hill of Saint Onofrio which was visible from the chapel, just as if he saw some great vision. On coming to the Gloria in Excelsis he began to sing, which was a very unusual thing for him, and he sung the whole of it with the greatest joy and devotion. Having finished his mass he gave communion to several; and after he had made his thanksgiving, they brought him a little broth, at which the Saint said, "They think that I am quite recovered, but it is not so." He then went again to the confessional, and received all who came with the greatest sweetness, caressing and embracing them more than usual.

Cardinal Agostino Cusano and Cardinal Federico Borromeo now came to see him on their return from the procession of the most holy Sacrament, and they remained talking of divine things with him till dinner time. As soon as the Cardinals had left him he took his usual collation, and after having reposed a short time, he said Vespers and Compline with more than ordinary devotion; the rest of the day he spent partly in receiving those who came to see him, of whom at parting he took his farewell in a very marked way, and partly in listening to the Lives of the Saints, which he had read to him, particularly that of S. Bernardine of Siena, which he had read over to him a second time. At five o'clock Cardinal Cusano came a second time, and with him Girolamo Panfilio, at that time Auditor of the Rota, and soon after came Pinello Benci, Bishop of Montepulciano, with whom Philip said the Matins of the following day, though the rest of that day's Office he was to finish with the angels and saints in Paradise. Having finished Matins, they left the place where they had said Office; and on Cardinal Cusano offering to assist Philip in mounting a staircase from the Loggia to his chamber, the Saint refused to let him, saying with a smile, "Do you think that I have not got quite strong again." When they had entered his room Angelo di Bagnarea, the medical man, came in and said, "Why, Father, you are better than you have ever been before; for these last ten years I have not seen you in such excellent health." The Saint afterwards heard the cardinal's confession, and on his taking his leave, the Saint, contrary to his usual custom, accompanied him to the staircase, pressing his hands strongly, and looking fixedly in his face as much as to say, "We shall never meet again." During the rest of the day down to supper-time he heard several other confessions. He afterwards supped alone, as was his usual custom; after supper he heard the confessions of those fathers who were to say the first masses on the following morning. After this many of those living in the house came according to their custom for his blessing, which he gave them, at the same time conversing with them in a familiar way with extraordinary sweetness.

At the third hour of the night he performed his usual spiritual exercises, and then got into bed in perfect health, without showing the slightest sign of sickness or infirmity. But he well knew that the hour of his death was now at hand, and therefore, as soon as he was in bed, he repeated with great earnestness those words which he had so often said of late, "Last of all, one must die." Shortly after he inquired what time it was; he was told it was the third hour of the night. Whereupon, as if talking to himself, he said, "Three and two are five, three and three are six, and then I shall go." He now laid himself down in the bed, and dismissed all who were with him, wishing to employ what little time remained to him in conversing with his Lord, whom he so ardently desired to meet. When it had struck five (of the night) he arose and began to walk up and down his room; on which Father Antonio Gallonio, who slept in the room below, ran up and found him lying again upon his bed, with such a violent cough and such an effusion of blood, that he had great reason to fear that it would choke him. Father Antonio asked him how he felt, and he replied, "Antonio, I am going." Father Antonio now ran to call for assistance, and sent off for the medical men; then returning with several others to the room of the Saint he found him sitting on the bed, in which posture he remained till his death. Thinking this attack was of the same nature as the previous ones, they applied what remedies they could, and succeeded in stopping the cough, so that in about a quarter of an hour the Saint seemed to have completely recovered, and he was able to speak distinctly. He, however, knew well that the moment of his death had now arrived, and therefore he said to them, "Do not trouble yourselves with applying remedies, for I am dying." Meantime all the fathers were called up to his room, and it seemed as if he was only waiting for them to arrive before he died.

They all knelt in front of his bed weeping, while Cesare Baronius, who was then superior, made the commendation of his soul, and being told by the medical man who stood by that the father was going, he said to him with a loud voice, "Father, are you going to leave us without saying a word to us? give us at least your blessing." At these words Philip lifted his hand slightly, and opening his eyes, which till then had remained closed, he raised them towards heaven, and kept them fixed there for some time; then lowering them towards the fathers who were kneeling round him he made a gentle inclination of the head towards them, as if he had obtained for them the blessing of God, and thus without another movement, but as if gently falling asleep, he expired.

Chapter 4 – Immediately after his death Philip appears to several persons

At the same hour at which he died Philip appeared to many persons, and first to Teo Guerra in Siena, to whom the holy father appeared as he was lying, between sleeping and waking, and fixing his eyes on him he said, "Peace be with thee, my brother; behold, I am going to a better place." At these words Teo Guerra awoke, and again heard them repeated three times, after which the vision disappeared. He afterwards received letters informing him that at that very time Philip had passed to a better life. Philip also appeared to a nun in the monastery of S. Cecilia in Trastevere, named Sister Ortenzia Anelli, who saw him carried by two angels in a seat covered with white, and she heard him say, "I am going to my rest; persevere in the labors of the religious life, for where I am going you also shall come, and doubt not but that I will pray to God for you much more now than formerly." At these words she awoke full of joy, marvelling greatly at the vision. In the morning she heard the news of the Saint's death, and perceived that it took place at the very time when she had seen the vision. He appeared at the same time to another nun, who was mistress of the novices in the convent of S. Maria Maddalena di Monte Cavallo, who on seeing him began to talk to him about her scruples, and wished to speak about the scruples of others; but the Saint said to her, "Let me go, for I cannot wait any longer, I have been detained too long by others." At this she awoke, and in the morning she received the news of his death.

Philip appeared on the same night to another nun, named Sister Vittoria de' Massimi, in the convent of S. Marta, who was a penitent of his, and said to her, "I have come to see you before I depart; you must not lament at losing me." The nun replied, "Ah father, are you then going to Paradise?" At this Philip showed her a field full of thorns, saying, "If you wish to come where I am going, you must pass through this," and immediately the nun awoke weeping and saying, "My father, I shall never see you more." Soon after this six hours of the night struck, and from that time to morning she did nothing but recommend herself to him, feeling sure that in the morning she should hear of his death; and so impressed was she with this belief, that whoever might have told her to the contrary she would not have believed them.

At Morlupo, a place about sixteen miles from Rome, there lived a virgin of the Third Order of S. Dominic, named Sister Caterina Paluzzi, a person of great perfection, whose Life has recently been published. She only knew of the Saint by report, and had not heard of his death, when having received the communion on the morning before the burial of the Saint, and being wide awake, there appeared to her a venerable old man dressed as a priest, clothed in white and shining like the sun. He was seated in a chair, and around his chair was a great space covered with diverse ornaments, on which were written in letters of gold the virtues in which this holy old man had most excelled. Around his chair but below him she saw a great number of souls of every state and condition, but none of them were so beautiful and resplendent as this old man. He was contemplating the most holy Trinity, and these souls were gazing on him. It seemed to her as if they were making a very sweet harmony like the singing and chanting of the angels, ascribing to him at the same time great glory and honor. She was desirous to know who these souls were, and she thereupon heard a voice that they were the souls of those who had been saved by means of this Saint. She related this vision to her spiritual director, Father David Negri, a Dominican, who made her give him a description of the appearance of the old man, and inquired what age be seemed to be of; all which she detailed with the utmost minuteness. The confessor hereupon showed her a portrait of the Saint which he had had taken during his lifetime; the instant she saw it she exclaimed, "This is the very same person that I saw in my Vision!"

A few days after the death of the Saint, Artemisia Cheli, a nun in the convent of the Purification at Rome, was talking to the reverend mother about the sanctity of Philip. "For my part," said she, "I believe that Father Philip was a great servant of God; but I should like to have seen him raise the dead, give light to the blind, and make the lame to walk; I should then have formed a higher opinion of him, and would have held for certain that he is a Saint. I know that he is reported to have done many, many miracles; still, partly because I have never witnessed any, and partly because there are so many stories of this kind about, which are full of exaggerations, I am not as yet altogether satisfied about his sanctity." The following night as she was sitting half asleep and half awake, so that she saw her sisters moving about the room, she had a vision in which she seemed to be in the church of S. Peter in Vaticano, under the cupola of which was a great platform, and on it she saw Philip; at the top of the cupola she saw a round table which shone very brightly. It seemed to her that the Saint said to her, "Artemisia, if you have not seen the things that I have done in my lifetime and since my death, see what I am going to do now." At these words he rose from the platform, ascended to the table and disappeared. Artemisia having awoke, and having reflected on what she had seen, and also on the words she had lately used about Philip, related the whole to the reverend mother, and repented that she had spoken so slightingly of the Saint. Very probably this apparition had some reference to the fact, that the Saint would one day be canonized in S. Peter's, after which no one would be allowed to entertain doubts as to his sanctity.

Chapter 5 – Of the concourse of people that came to see the Saint's body before it was buried

At the seventh hour of the night the body having been washed and clad in the priestly vestments, was carried into the church accompanied by all the fathers and brethren of the Congregation. The church was opened very early the next morning, and the news of his death having been spread throughout Rome, the church was quickly thronged with persons of every condition of life. The body seemed to be surrounded by an indescribable air of sanctity, and the face in particular attracted the eyes of all, for it was so beautiful that it seemed quite to shine. The funeral obsequies were performed, and the Office of the Dead was recited, after which solemn Mass of the Dead was sung, at which several prelates assisted.

Whilst they were reciting the Office of the Dead, a cleric, named Antonio Carrari, and a penitent of Philip's, came in; he was suffering at the time from a great anxiety of mind, but putting on a cotta in order to go into choir to recite Office with the others, he earnestly recommended himself to the Saint, and was immediately delivered from it.

Many cardinals came to see his body, and among them came Cardinal Agostino Cusano, and Cardinal Frederic Borromeo, who with many tears kissed both his hands and feet. Cardinal Gabriello Paleotto also came, and saw now to his great sorrow him dead whom in his book, "De Bono Senectutis," he had taken as a perfect example of a holy old man. Cardinal Ottavio Paravicino, who loved him tenderly, was almost inconsolable. Many of the nobility also came to the church to venerate the body of the saint, among whom was the Duchess of Sessa, the wife of the Spanish Ambassador. We must not forget to relate how Baronius, thinking within himself what kind of prayer he had better say for Philip in private, could not decide whether it would be right to say the De Profundis for him as for other deceased persons. He therefore recommended the matter to God, and begged that he would make His

Will known to him; on opening his Breviary, his eye rested on these words of the Psalm, "Respice de coelo, et vide et visita vineam istam et perfice eam quam plantavit dextera tua." The fathers therefore, at the suggestion of Baronius, made use of these words for some time privately among themselves, in order to recommend their affairs to Philip. A similar thing happened to Marcello Vitelleschi, who was lying ill in bed when the news of Philip's death was brought to him, he also could not bring himself to say the De Profundis for him, but said the Laudate Dominum omnes gentes instead, which is usually said to commemorate the souls of infants. In the same way some religious wishing to say the Mass of Requiem for him, said the Mass de Gloria instead, and many others said the Gloria Patri at the end of the Psalms instead of, as they intended, the Requiem aeternam. The Abbate Crescenzio in saying for him, also felt a notable repugnance to say the Mass of Requiem.

Fra. Girolamo Beger, a Dominican and Preacher-general of his Order, of whom we have already spoken, preached a sermon the same day in praise of Philip, in the church of the Minerva. He said that it was unnecessary to pray for Philip dead, since he was living amidst the glories of Paradise, and that the Masses of Requiem that were said for the soul of Philip would be of avail to other souls in purgatory, but not to his. Many also said that the Pope would canonize him immediately, and that he would thus also enjoy that glory on earth, which they held for certain he was now enjoying in heaven.

During the two days in which the body remained in the church, there was a continued stream of people who came to see it, and to kiss the hands or the feet; many persons out of devotion touched the body with their rosaries, and others who could not get close to it contented themselves with kissing the bier. Some persons cut off pieces of his vestments, though the fathers did all they could to hinder this; others cut off some of his hair, or of his beard, and some cut portions of his finger-nails, which they afterwards kept by them as relics.

Many ladies came, and out of devotion drew their rings from their fingers and put them on the fingers of the Saint, after which they replaced them on their own. The flowers which were strewed over the Saint's body were also carried off, so that they had to put fresh ones there several times, but each time they were carried off by the people.

Besides secular persons great numbers of religious also came to kiss his hands; amongst them came the Master of Novices among the Dominicans, with the whole novitiate, who standing in a circle round the bier, now took their last look at that father from whom when living they had often received such great spiritual consolation.

Among the crowd persons of every rank and condition were heard lamenting the death of the Saint, and recounting his different virtues. Some expressed their grief at losing such a wonderful example of sanctity; others, considering the great fruit that had been produced by the Exercises, not only in Rome, but also in many other parts of Christendom, declared that undoubtedly a great light of the Church of God was now extinguished. Others again said that Philip was indeed a great man, for although he had such constant intercourse with the most exalted personages and with so many of the supreme Pontiffs, yet he had lived entirely free from any spirit of ambition. Many were heard praising his great humility, which had enabled him so successfully to conceal his sanctity, and in particular to conceal the miracles which he used daily to work. Some again blessed and praised him for having instituted the Oratory; but above all, the poor lamented him, who had so frequently relieved their wants, and they were heard exclaiming that the father of the poor was dead. All, in fine, who had known him in his lifetime, when they looked upon his face, and remembered how kindly and lovingly he used to converse with them, were unable to refrain from weeping at seeing themselves henceforth deprived of this.

Chapter 6 – Of the miracles which were worked before the body was buried

Whilst the holy body was thus lying exposed in the church, God was pleased to magnify his servant yet more by miracles immediately after his death. There was a boy about eleven years of age, named Agostino de Magistris, who for six or seven years past had been suffering from a scrofulous affection in his throat, for which he had been attended by all the first surgeons in Rome; he had also an ulcer inside his mouth, which extended completely across it from one side to the other. On the day of the Saint's death this boy was at school with several others, when he heard someone say that a holy father was dead at the Chiesa Nuova, who was working miracles. Upon this he went off immediately to the church, and having with great difficulty contrived to get close up to the bier, he first made a little prayer, and then with great faith touched his throat with the hand of the Saint, and was immediately cured, so that before leaving the church he took off the plaster which he wore, and on his arrival at home there was no mark or sign of the sore to be seen, and the ulcer in his mouth had entirely disappeared. Cardinal Paleotto, when he heard of the miracle, sent for the boy, and with his own hands touched the place where the sore had been, and finding that the boy was really perfectly cured he was greatly edified, and praised the majesty of God, who is continually showing Himself to be wonderful in His saints. Agostino, on his return home, related the whole story to his mother. Now her daughter, who was younger than Agostino, had also been afflicted for six years past with a similar affection on both sides of her throat. The mother therefore took her to the Chiesa Nuova, and lifting her up on the bier she touched the child's throat with the hands of the Saint on one side only, not being able to touch both sides because of the great crowd, and also because she had to make way for the wife of the Spanish Ambassador, who had just arrived in the church; the child's throat, however, was immediately cured. She was also prevented thus from touching as she wished one of the child's legs in the same way, which for two years had been so weak that the child could not stand upon it. She therefore took some of the roses from the bier, and at night made a bath with them, into which she put the child's leg, and immediately she was able to walk and stand upon it, and the leg became quite sound and strong. Alessandro, the father of these children, who was about sixty years old, had for two months been suffering from a weakness in his eyes, which caused them to water so much that at night he could not bear a light in his room. From the quantity of moisture that constantly flowed from his eyes he feared that eventually he should become blind; on hearing of the death of Philip, however, he went off in great faith to see the body; and having taken the hand of the Saint he applied it to his eyes, which became better immediately, and without any assistance from physicians in a short time he was completely freed from the disease.

At the same time a son of Pietro Contini, named Angelo, was lying ill of a sharp fever, which was attended with great pain; the disease had taken such hold upon him that he was given over by the physicians. It happened that one of his brothers went to see the body of the Saint before it was buried, and taking some of the flowers which were strewn over the Saint's chasuble, he returned home and placed them with great faith upon the head of his sick brother. At the same instant their mother came into the room, and seeing her son lying with his face nearly black and apparently dead, she went aside to another room to weep. Her other son followed her, and told her what he had just done with the flowers; upon this the mother returned, and found that the blackness had quite disappeared from the face of Angelo, and that it had recovered its natural expression; and whereas he had for some time neither spoken nor shown any sign of consciousness, he now began to laugh and play with his brothers, and the confessor arriving just at this moment to give him Extreme Unction, to his great astonishment found him perfectly cured. Epifania Colicchia of Recanati had been afflicted for seven months with an asthma, which was so bad that she could scarcely draw her breath, and at night she was unable to sleep, and she could not bear to lie down or to walk, and thus she remained in constant pain. On hearing that

Father Philip at the Chiesa Nuova was dead and was working miracles, she set off for the church, and kneeling down there she prayed for some time, begging the Saint with many tears to restore her to health; then taking some of the roses which were strewed over the body, she applied them to her stomach and was instantaneously delivered from the asthma, and from all the pain she had till that time endured, not having applied any other remedy either before or after. At the same time she was cured of a sore which was so bad that it had made the flesh all round as black as ink, and it was attended with excessive pain. The instant the place was touched with the roses the matter began to dry up, and in a few days the spot was quite clean and pure as if there had never been any sore at all.

Maria Giustiniani, a girl of noble family, suffered from great pains in the head, which medical skill had entirely failed to cure. She was taken by her mother to see the body of the Saint, and when they got up to the bier the mother secretly cut off some of the Saint's hair and returned home with it, feeling assured that she had now obtained a remedy for her daughter. She therefore rubbed the head of her daughter with the hair, saying, "O St. Philip, by the desire which thou always hadst to assist others, I beseech thee now to heal my daughter;" at the same instant her daughter began to amend, and in a short time was perfectly well. Dorotea Brumani had a son rather more than two years old, whose legs were so weak and his knees turned in in such a way that he was quite unable to walk, and it was necessary for him to be always carried in arms or to be sitting down; and although she had often endeavored to make him walk, she was not even able to make him stand upright, and the various remedies which she had applied were all unavailing. She had often wished to get Philip to lay his hand on the child's head, but had never had an opportunity; still, she always entertained a firm confidence that if the servant of God were to die, and she could succeed in touching his body with her son's legs, she should obtain his cure. Immediately, therefore, that she heard of his death, she ordered the nurse to take the child to the church, and she followed shortly after them. Having arrived at the church she took the child from his nurse's arms, and drawing off his stockings touched the Saint's body with both his legs, and then sent him home, while she remained in the church to pray. On her return the nurse came out to meet her, and told her that the child was walking, and the mother on entering the house found that it was so, and from that time forward the child became perfectly strong and healthy, and was everafter able to walk without feeling any weakness whatever.

Artemisia Cheli had a swelling in her left hand just at the joint, which the surgeons said was a knot or tumor, and this gradually increased in size till it became as large as an egg. She had suffered from it for two years, when on hearing of the Saint's death she came to the church, and taking some of the roses that were strewed over the body, she began to rub the place with them, and in a short time, almost without her perceiving it, the swelling entirely disappeared.

Chapter 7 – Of what happened when Philip's body was opened, and of his burial

On the evening of the 26th of May, the body having been exposed the whole day in the church, at about three hours of the night the physicians and surgeons were called in to open it, and many members of the Congregation were present: and now a wonderful thing occurred, for when in turning the body they might have seen even those parts which modesty usually conceals, the Saint with his own hand sheltered and protected himself from the eyes of the beholders in the same way as a living man would. Angelo da Bagnarea perceiving this turned full of astonishment to the bystanders, and said, "See how this father who was so chaste in life, shows himself so even after death." The same thing had happened when the fathers were washing the body, and every one understood it to be a sign of his virginity and singular purity. They also observed that the body did not give out the slightest fetid smell as dead bodies generally do, and they were the more astonished at this because the weather was remarkably hot, indeed, many persons declared that a sweet and pleasant smell came from it. When they had opened the body they found the swelling under his left breast was occasioned by two of his ribs which were broken, as we have already mentioned in speaking of the palpitation of his heart. They found the praecordia sound and quite free from disease; his heart was unusually large; there was no water in the pericardium, and no blood in the ventricles of the heart; the great artery was of about twice the ordinary size, and from this the medical men and surgeons inferred that the ardor of his continual contemplation must have been excessive.

For the consolation of those who from their devotion to Philip were desirous of having a likeness of him, the fathers had a cast of his face taken in plaster of Paris, and from this mold many other casts were taken in wax, which were exact representations of him. Philip was of middle stature; of a fair complexion, and of a cheerful countenance; in his youth his features were very beautiful; his forehead was high and broad but not bald; his nose aquiline; his eyes small and of a blue color, rather sunk but of a very lively expression; his beard was black and not very long, but in the last years of his life it became quite white.

The medical men having finished their operations, the body was again placed on the bier, and was exposed to the people the whole of the next day; on the evening of the 27th of May the fathers by common consent ordered that it should be placed in a common coffin, and buried in the common burying-place of the Congregation beneath the choir. Cardinal Federico Borromeo, on hearing of this, thought it was not right that so great a man should be buried in this way; he therefore remonstrated with the fathers, and also with Alessandro, the Cardinal of Florence. The latter agreed that it was not right to put him in the common burial-place, and said that even if the fathers did not wish to take on themselves to declare him to be a Saint, they ought nevertheless to have placed his body in some place apart, in order to see what God might be pleased to do with regard to the canonization of His servant. The body was therefore removed and placed in a walnut coffin, on which was a brass plate with his name engraved, and it was then deposited in a little chapel above the first arch of the nave of the church on the epistle side, as we have already mentioned, and above the coffin they built a sloping wall. It was considered very remarkable, that when they removed the body there was no offensive smell, and all his limbs were perfectly flexible, especially his hands, nor was there any sign of corruption visible; his face was very beautiful, and there appeared in it a certain grave and noble air, so that it seemed as if he were asleep.

The people immediately began to frequent the place where his body had thus been deposited, and numbers of votive offerings were placed there. Many persons perceived a very sweet fragrance proceeding from the spot, amongst others, Giulia Orsina Marchesa Rangona, a woman of great piety, who used often to come and pray to the Saint under that arch; at which times she often smelt so sweet an odor that she was greatly consoled by it. The smell was like that of roses and other flowers, which at that particular time were not in bloom. It is impossible to count the numbers who by simply visiting the tomb felt their heart lightened and their devotion greatly increased. We must not omit to relate how that eight months' afterwards, that is to say, on the 26th of January, 1596, Cardinal Cusano having a great desire to possess some relic of Philip, obtained permission to have his praecordia, which had been buried separately, disinterred. Although they had been placed in a common earthen vessel without a lid, and covered with earth, yet when they were taken up in presence of the cardinal they were found to be quite fresh and white, without the slightest mark of corruption or any bad smell, as though they had been but just buried. They were carefully washed with rose-water, and then put to dry in the sun; portions of them were afterwards distributed to different persons, and a part was placed in a very rich reliquary of silver. Some rags also with which the holy father used to dress an issue which he had in one of his arms, exhaled a most fragrant smell, although stained with matter and blood, so that being thrown aside after his death, in order that they might be washed and afterwards kept as relics, they lay there for some time quite forgotten, but being found some time after quite foul and dirty, they gave out such a sweet smell, that instead of provoking disgust they excited great devotion as well as astonishment in the hearts of all present.

Chapter 8 – Seven years after his death the body of S. Philip is translated to his little chapel

Nero del Nero had always a great devotion to the holy father, and he counted it as a great honor to have conversed with him and to have known him intimately, declaring that whenever the holy old man embraced him, which he used to do every time that he saw him suffering from any passion, he felt his heart consoled and comforted, and bursting into tears he used to find himself freed from the temptation. The same thing happened to him also many times after the death of Philip on visiting his tomb, where he used often to go and pray. This gentleman, as he was very rich and had no son, wished to make a grand coffin of silver for the holy body. The fathers first of all, therefore, thought it prudent to examine and see what state the body was in; for this purpose, on the 7th of March, 1599, after it had remained four years in the place we have described, they pulled down the wall and opened the coffin. They found the body covered with cobwebs and dust, which had got in through a crack in the lid of the coffin, caused by the moisture in the wall which had been built over it; his vestments were like so much dirt, and the chasuble had become so rotten that it all fell to pieces, and the plate on which his name was engraved was covered with verdigris, so that they expected to find his body reduced to dust. On the following evening, however, having removed all the rubbish, they found not only his legs and arms entire, but even the breast and stomach so fresh and beautiful, and the skin and flesh so moist, that everyone was astonished: the breast, moreover, retained its natural color and whiteness. This was considered by Andrea Cesalpino, Antonio Porto, and Ridolfo Silvestri, three of the first medical men of the time, to be undoubtedly miraculous; and they all three wrote upon the subject, showing that neither by nature nor by any artificial means could that body have been preserved in that manner without the especial aid of Divine Omnipotence. It was no less remarkable, that on opening the coffin and on removing the decayed vestments, no smell of putrefaction was perceived, so that the holy body, instead of exciting any horror or disgust, moved all to love, and reverence, and devotion. The Abbate Giacomo Crescenzio, one of Philip's spiritual children, had a new coffin made of cypress wood richly adorned, and on the evening of the 13th of May the body was taken out of the old coffin and placed in the new one on a little mattress of red taffety, and covered with a quilt of the same color. All the fathers and brethren of the house came to see the body of their holy father, weeping for joy, and congratulating one another on the possession of such a treasure. Alessandro Medici, Cardinal of Florence, Cardinal Federico Borromeo, and Cardinal Cesare Baronio, were also present. The Cardinal of Florence ordered new vestments to be made, and on the 21st of the month of May, they again clothed him in the priestly vestments, and put on him the chasuble in which he said mass on the day he died. The same Cardinal put a garland on his head, and drawing from his own finger a pontifical ring, in which was a very fine sapphire, he placed it on the finger of Philip; he also had a quantity of artificial flowers of silk strewed over the body, and on the breast was placed a silver crucifix, presented for this purpose by Giulio Sansedonio, Bishop of Grosseto, another of the Saint's spiritual children, and one much beloved by him. After this the holy body was again deposited in the same chapel over the arch of the church, where it remained till the 24th of May, 1602. The face having been a little injured, they had a silver mask made from the cast which had been taken, and this they put over the face, thereby verifying, though without thinking of it, what the holy father had said on one occasion in the house of a noble man, namely, that his head should be placed in silver.

Meanwhile Nero del Nero, of whom we have just been speaking, having chosen Philip as the especial and perpetual protector of himself and his posterity, and having obtained the consent of Elizabetta, the Saint's sister, who was then eighty-four years old, and the only heir of his house, by a public instrument and with all the necessary formalities, united his family with that of Philip, and annexed the arms of the Saint, namely, azure, three stars of, to his own. As he had no male child he had recourse to Philip's prayers, and through the merits of the Saint, at the end of nine months God gave him a son, whom he named Philip, in acknowledgment of the grace he had received, and who was afterwards the heir to all his property, and had a very great devotion to the holy father. Moreover, out of gratitude for this and the many other benefits which he had received through the Saint's intercession, Nero changed his design of having a silver coffin made into something which would tend more to the glory of God and to the Saint's honor. On the 6th of July, therefore, in the year 1600, he commenced building a magnificent chapel, the same which now exists, and which he adorned with precious stones and with all possible splendor. The walls are all encrusted with jasper, agate, and other precious stones, and the cupola is supported by four columns of alabaster, adorned with roses of mother-of-pearl and gold mouldings, with the ground of ultramarine blue. The pavement is conformable to the cupola, and is made of roses of alabaster and other stones; in the middle is a very large green oriental jasper with other jaspers, and the vestibule of the chapel is also adorned with the same precious stones. Cardinal Francesco Maria Tarugi laid the first stone, and he placed under it twelve brass medals and one large one of silver, bearing the likeness of S. Philip, with the inscription, "B. Philippus Nerius Florentinus, Congregationis Oratorii Fundator, obiit Romae anno millesimo quingentesimo nonagesimo quinto." A great plate of lead was put with the medals, with these words engraved on it: "This chapel was founded in honor of the Blessed Philip Neri of Florence, Founder of the Congregation of the Oratory, by Nerus de Nigris, a noble Florentine, at his own expense, in the year of the Jubilee, one thousand six hundred, in the month of July, on the octave of the feast of the holy apostles Peter and Paul, in the ninth year of the pontificate of Pope Clement VIII."

While the chapel was in the course of erection, it pleased God to allow the child that had been obtained through the intercession of the Saint, to fall dangerously ill of the smallpox. The disease became so serious that the child lost his voice, could scarcely breathe, and was quite given over by the physicians, so that his death was hourly expected. Nero, his father, not wishing to see him die, went into another room, where, throwing himself on a bed, he exclaimed full of anguish, "O holy father, must it be then that the first ceremony in the chapel I am building in thy honor is to be the funeral of my son, and that my only one!" He had scarcely said the words when the child, as if waking out of sleep, cried out three or four times, "Papa! Papa!" The Countess of Pitigliano, his sister, who was in the room, immediately ran to her father, and brought him to the child; when the child saw him he said distinctly, so that all could hear him, "Papa, I am cured, and godfather has cured me;" for so he called the holy father, because as he was named after him in baptism they often showed him a picture of the Saint, and told him that it was his godfather. In order to make the matter more certain, they asked him if it was his godmother that had cured him, but he cried out louder than ever, "No, no, it was godfather," and on their showing him the picture he said that this was the person he meant. When they asked him how he had been cured, the child touched his head, meaning that by touching his head the Saint had cured him. Having taken a little broth, he began to suck and then fell asleep; during his sleep a quantity of matter began to distil from his ears, showing that an abscess had burst in his head; this discharge continued for some days, after which the child became quite strong and well. This new benefit made Nero more anxious than ever for the completion of the chapel. At length, on the 24th of May, 1601, seven years after the death of the Saint, his body was translated with great reverence and devotion into the new chapel, several cardinals and prelates being present, although it was done privately and with closed doors. Early in the morning on the day appointed, which was Friday, the body was taken by a number of priests in cottas and with lighted torches, and singing psalms and hymns, and carried into the sacristy, where it remained all day surrounded by a number of lighted candles. In the evening, after the Ave, the doors were shut to avoid there being a concourse of people, though a great number were present notwithstanding, to each of whom was given a large wax taper. The body was then carried in procession round the church accompanied by numbers of priests and clerics in cottas and bearing lighted torches; the church as well as the chapel was full of lights and flowers and perfumes; immediately after the bier came Cardinal Francesco Maria Tarugi, Cardinal Cesare Baronio and Monsignor Panfilio, who was afterwards Cardinal. The body was then placed in the middle of the chapel, and after the Te Deum had been sung, and certain prayers recited, it was finally deposited in the place prepared for it in the said chapel; next morning, mass was said there for the first time by Cardinal Tarugi, and from that time forward it has been said there daily.

In the year 1639, when the coffin of cypress wood was again opened, in order to take out some relics to send to the fathers of the Congregation at Naples, the holy body was again found incorrupt; after which it was enclosed in another coffin of iron, made to close in such a way that it could not be opened again, and this was then covered with silver. The following inscription was at the same time placed on the tomb: "Corpus S. Philippi Nerii Congregationis Oratorii Fundatoris Ab Ipso Dormitionis Die Annos Quatuor et Quadraginta Incorruptum Divina Virtute Servatum Oculis Fidelium Expositum A dilectis in Christo Filiis, Sub Ejusdem Patris Altari Perpetuae Sepulturae More Majorum Commendatum Est Anno Salutis MDCXXXVIII. Urbani Papae XVIII. XVI. Indictione VII. Idibus Aprilis."

Chapter 9 – Honors paid to Philip after his death

The opinion of Philip's sanctity increased so much after his death by reason of the miracles worked through his intercession, that votive offerings began almost immediately to be sent to his tomb, although the fathers refused to receive them, and did all in their power to prevent their being sent. The Abbate Marco Antonio Maffa, Apostolic Visitor and Examiner of Bishops, sent the first offering, which he fixed up with his own hand, together with a candle. His reason for doing so was this: some few weeks after the Saint's death he was seized with a pestilential fever and lethargy which would not yield to the treatment of the physicians. While he was lying in this state he had the following vision. It seemed that the house in which he lived was on fire, and that persons outside were trying to throw down the walls; on this two strong young men who were with him ran as quickly as they could to the door to avoid the danger, but just as they reached the door that part of the wall fell on them and killed them both. He himself was terribly alarmed, when on a sudden he saw the holy father, who seemed very angry with the others, and cried out, "Save the Abbate! Save the Abbate!" at which words he seemed to be instantaneously delivered from his danger. Immediately after this vision he began to grow better, and on the following day he had perfectly recovered and was quite free from the fever. In testimony of the grace he had received, he hung up the tablet we have just mentioned over the Saint's tomb, and underneath it he placed the following inscription:-

"J. C. R.
B. Philippo Liberatori Suo
Id. Anton. Maffa Presb. Salernit.
Non. Aug. M. D. XC. V.

Cum me febris vehementissima invassisset, videbar noctu in domo recina et incendio conclusus, nullum habens evadendi diffugium. Duo qui videbantur mecum esse, fuga sibi consulentes, a pariete oppressi mortui sunt. Dam in metu perterritus mortem expectarem, vidi at audivi B. Philippum iterato praecipientem iis qui domum disjiciebant, his verbis, Salvate Abbatem. Postridie reliquit me febris, quod illius meritis et precibus acceptum fereus, testatum volui hac tabella, in nomine Patris, et Filii et Spiritus Sancti, et ad honorem ejusdem Beati Philippi. Amen."

The same Abbate was the first who suspended a lighted lamp before the tomb; and when it was removed by the orders of the Fathers, he went and complained to his Holiness, Clement VIII, and obtained his permission to have it restored, which it was a few days after. A noble lady, named Costanza del Drago, seeing this, also presented a silver lamp of great value, and by degrees the others were given which are now to be seen in the chapel.

The same year in which the Saint died, a portrait of him was published by the permission of superiors, with the title of "Blessed," and surrounded with rays and representations of his miracles; his picture was also to be seen in many palaces and private houses. Many persons had copies taken from the cast which had been made of his face after death, and these they kept in their rooms with great devotion. Clement VIII had one standing on a little table, besides his portrait, which he kept in his room covered with a veil along with several other portraits of Saints. It would be impossible to tell the number of those who immediately after his death prayed to him and honored him as a Saint; his tomb was visited from the very first by many cardinals and prelates, by great numbers of the nobility and of persons in every rank of life. So great was the devotion they had to him, that they used to kiss the wall which contained his coffin; many of them took away with them some of the dust from the wall or from the ground in front of it; several prelates also took some of the oil from the lamp that burnt before the tomb; others carried off the flowers which were frequently strewed there, carrying them about with them as relics, and oftentimes they received great favors from the Lord by means of them. Many persons out of devotion used to come and make a visit to the tomb every day, and some of these, even persons of quality, used to come barefoot.

The year after his death, on the day of his anniversary, instead of the mass of Requiem they sung the mass of the day, and had a very grand function, at which many cardinals and prelates assisted, and there was a great concourse of people present. In the evening after Vespers there was a sermon in praise of him. Similar sermons were preached on the following day, some of them by members of the Congregation, and some by prelates and others. Three years after the Saint's death, Clement VIII gave permission for mass to be celebrated in the room of the holy father, which had been converted into a chapel; the same altar being placed in it at which he himself used to say mass when living. Above it was painted a picture of Philip in the act of recommending the Congregation to the Blessed Virgin, and round the walls were pictures representing some of his principal miracles, together with other ornaments. The rooms which he used to occupy at S. Girolamo della Carità were also converted into a chapel.

Many also were the encomiums paid to Philip by different writers; Cardinal Gabriello Paleotto, in his book *"De Bono Senectutis,"* speaking of the opinion people had of Philip's sanctity, adds, "This much, kind reader, we had written and reduced to its present form long since, so that it only remained to be printed; when, behold, the man of God by the dispensation of him who governs all things, fell sick, although he was not thereby confined to his bed or hindered from performing his ordinary duties. On the 26th of May, however, he was suddenly taken from us, being called from his exile to enter his heavenly country. Although his death was quite unlooked for by us, still we have determined not to change the plan we had fixed on, namely, to propose this excellent old man as a living picture by which we might teach the virtues of old age; for although it is now four months since he was taken from us, and since he has disappeared from our eyes as one that is dead, he still is living in heaven the life of the living, as his holy and wonderful words testify: he still lives here on earth in the memory of the just and good, above all in this city of Rome, where he has left so many spiritual children whom he has begotten in Christ." Farther on he adds, "Wherefore hoping that by reason of the many wonderful works that he has done and is doing, his name will every day become more known and better known to all, we have had his likeness here engraved, both for the consolation of those who knew and loved him as their father in Christ, and also in order that those who shall hereafter hear of his name, may become the more inflamed with a desire to imitate him; and, finally, in order that those who come after us may have perpetually before their eyes a picture, by looking on which they may learn to know the virtues of old age, and knowing them may pay them due respect." Thus far Cardinal Gabriello Paleotto.

Cardinal Frederico Borromeo, in a letter to Father Antonio Gallonio, writes as follows: "You know how much I honor this Saint, you know my love for him. Since his death this has not diminished but increased, and if necessary I would shed my blood for his sake." Cardinal Agostino Cusano says of him, "Thus it hath pleased God, after eighty years spent in His service, to call to Himself that holy soul adorned with so many Christian virtues. We may apply to him those words of scripture: 'Qui ad justitiam erudiunt multos, fulgebunt quasi stellae in perpetuas aeternitates;' and also those words of the Psalm, 'Longitudine dierum replebo eum, et ostendam illi salutare meum.'" This Cardinal's devotion towards the Saint was so great, that in addition to the many tokens he gave of it in his lifetime, he began his will when on his deathbed with these words: "First, I commend my soul with all humility of heart into the hands of our most merciful Lord Jesus Christ, and to the hands of His most holy Mother the Virgin Mary, to the glorious princes of the apostles saints Peter and Paul, S. Augustine and S. Francis, and to the Blessed Philip, and to all the saints; in order that it may be made worthy of the divine mercy, and of their fellowship in the life to come," &c.

Cardinal Ottavio Bandini, beholding in Philip, as it were at one view, all the virtuous actions which he performed during his whole life, speaks of him as follows: "It seems to me that in Philip were united all the good qualities, all the virtues, all the prerogatives, and all the circumstances, which we are accustomed to admire separately in the lives and deaths of the other Saints canonized by the Holy Church." Cardinal Cesare Baronio also in his Annotations to the Martyrology under the 23rd of August, speaking of S. Philip Benizi of Florence, the Institutor of the Order of Servites, takes occasion to praise Philip, by saying, "The city of Florence is adorned with two Philips, the one the Institutor of the Servites, the other the Founder of the Oratory, and the many miracles which are worked daily at the intercession of the latter, show clearly that he too as well as the first is reigning gloriously in heaven." Cardinal Girolamo Panfilio says of him, "Every day the fame of this blessed father increases through the great number of miracles which are worked in favor of those who invoke him; I myself in particular am daily receiving favors from him, and I trust that he will constantly assist me for the future in everything; for I have put myself completely and entirely under his protection, and from the bottom of my heart I beg him to take charge of me."

Many others wrote concerning the virtues of Philip, in particular Rutilio Benzoni, Bishop of Loreto and Recanati, in his book, De Anno Sancto Jubilaei; and Giovan Battista del Tufo, Bishop of Cerra, in the Annals of the Clerks Regular; Don Silvano Razzi, in his Collection of the Lives of the Saints of Tuscany, inserted at the end that of the Blessed Philip. The same was done by Alfonso Vigliega, in his Collection of the Lives of the Saints. Father Arcangelo Giani, of the Order of Servites, speaks in praise of Philip in his Life of S. Philip Benizi; so also does Tommaso Bozzio, in his book, De Signis Ecclesiae Dei, et de ruinis gentium; and also Francesco Bocchi, in his Praises of Celebrated Persons born in Florence. His Life was also translated into several languages, amongst others into the dialect of Castile, by Monsignor Lodovico Crespi, Bishop of Placenza, who was Ambassador Extraordinary from his Catholic Majesty to his Holiness Alexander VII, and who was very instrumental in obtaining the bull which that Pope issued concerning the Conception of the Blessed Virgin. In the year 1665, Monsignor Andrea di Saussay, Bishop and Count of Tulle, published a Latin Compendium of the Saint's Life, together with some very erudite annotations on the bull of his canonization; besides many other translations by different persons, which to avoid tediousness I omit.

Many memorials of him were also set up, in particular Guilio Sansedonio, afterwards Bishop of Grosseto, and at that time presiding over the church of San Girolamo della Carità, had a representation of S. Philip in the act of recommending his spiritual children to the Blessed Virgin, painted in the Cortile of that place. Under it he placed the following inscription: "Beato Philippo Nerio Florentino. Ut ubi triginta tres annos eximia sanctitatis et miraculorum laude claruerat, innumerisque ad Christi obsequium traducti s, prima Congregationis fundamenta jecerat, ibi aliquod ejus rei monumentum extaret; Templi hujus domus, ac Sacerdotum Deputatus annuente pissima Congregatione Charitatis, Parenti in spiritu optimo benemerenti posuit. Kal. Septembris MDCV." At the same time many offerings were sent to his tomb. Cardinal Agostino Cusano sent a pall of brocade to adorn it. Alfonso Visconte, Bishop of Cervia, and after cardinal, also sent a very rich piece of drapery for the same purpose; it was of crimson velvet, embroidered with gold and worked with flowers, being part of the spoils taken from Sisan Bassà, the Turkish admiral. In consequence of the ever-increasing opinion of the sanctity of Philip, the Roman people ordered by a public decree, that every year on the 26th of May, that being the Feast of the Saint, the magistrates should solemnly present a silver chalice and four torches in his chapel. Duke Maximilian of Bavaria also sent a lamp of silver worth a thousand scudi, to burn for ever before his tomb, as it does to this day. Charles of Lorraine sent another of great value, and many other precious gifts have been made by different cardinals, prelates, and others.

Five years after the death of Philip, his Life, in which he was entitled Blessed, was published by permission of Pope Clement; it was written in Latin and in the Vernacular, and was composed by Father Antonio Gallonio. The same Pope Clement used to take great pleasure in hearing it read to him. Besides this it was approved by many of the cardinals, who subscribed these words: "All the things which are here related of the Blessed Philip Neri, I, N. declare in part to have witnessed with my own eyes, and in part to have learnt upon the undoubted testimony of grave and trustworthy persons," &c.

On the death of Clement VIII he was succeeded by Leo XI, who when he was urged to canonize S. Charles, especially by Cardinal Baronio, replied that he was willing to canonize S. Charles, but that he wished also to canonize the Blessed Philip. Inasmuch, however, as God had granted him only a short life, he was unable to carry out his wish. After him Paul V was raised to the Pontificate, and he showed in what veneration he held the Saint by beatifying him, as we shall see in the following chapter, and by granting his Office and Mass to all the Congregations, on which occasion his picture painted by Guido Reni was exposed in his chapel in the position in which it is to be seen at this day, to the great consolation of the holy father's children, who had so much desired it; besides which, long before he beatified him, the same Pope several times granted, vive vocis oraculo, a plenary indulgence on the day of his feast. The devotion which Gregory XV had for Philip was well known to all who conversed with him about the Saint when he was Auditor of the Rota; after he was made Cardinal he said once in a letter, that if it should ever please the Divine Majesty to raise him to the See of Peter, he would certainly canonize Philip, which he accordingly did.

Chapter 10 – Of the canonization of Philip, and of the acts made for that purpose

In order to give a clear account of the progress and order of the canonization of Philip, so that all who read his Life may see with what caution and discretion the Holy Roman Church proceeds in the canonization of saints, we will here make mention of all that was done in the matter from the time of Philip's death to the day when he was inscribed in the Catalogue of Saints by Gregory XV of glorious memory.

Shortly after the death of Philip several persons, and in particular the Abbate Marco Antonio Maffa, being moved by the constantly increasing opinion of his sanctity, in consequence of his virtues and miracles, earnestly besought his Holiness that he would allow a Process to be formed relating to the actions, virtues, and miracles of Philip. In reply to this Clement VIII, who was then Pope, crossing his hands three times on his breast, uttered these formal words: "We hold him to be a saint." Shortly after this he gave orders, vive vocis oraculo, to Lodovico de Torres, at that time Archbishop of Monreale, and afterwards Cardinal, and to Audoeno Lodovico, Bishop of Cassano, both of them Apostolic Visitors, that they should have a Process formed upon the virtues and miracles of Philip. These last, at the instance of Cardinal Agostino Cusano, and of Cesare Baronio, at that time Superior of the Congregation, ordered Giacomo Buzio, a canon of S. John Lateran and notary of Cardinal Girolamo Rusticucci, the Pope's vicar, to examine witnesses and receive evidence for that purpose.

The first Process, then, was commenced on the 2nd of August, 1595, that is, two months after the death of the Saint, and the examination was continued with the greatest diligence and accuracy down to the 1st of June, 1601. At that time Giacomo Buzio died, and Cardinal Francesco Maria Tarugi, Cardinal Cesare Baronio, Apostolical Librarian, and Flaminio Ricci, Superior of the Congregation, made fresh entreaties that the Process which had been commenced might be carried on and completed, so that it might be laid up in the Vatican Library as a perpetual memorial of the sanctity of Philip.

On the 8th of February, therefore, 1605, Cardinal Camillo Borghese, who was then the Papal Vicar, and afterwards Paul V, gave orders to his notary, Pietro Maggiotti, to go on receiving evidence, and to bring the said Process to a conclusion. He accordingly began to examine witnesses on the 12th of February, 1605, and on the 21st of September in the same year the Process was completed. In the course of it more than three hundred and sixty persons were examined on the usual oath, among whom were cardinals, prelates, and other persons of title. It was laid up by Cardinal Baronio in the Vatican Library. This is the first Process, made as they say with ordinary authority.

The first Process having been completed, in the year 1608 Charles Gonzaga, Duke of Nevers, came to Rome as Ambassador Extraordinary to his holiness, Pope Paul V from his most Christian Majesty King Henry IV; and he went to visit the tomb of the Blessed Philip, because he had at one time gone to confession to him, and because he knew him to be a man of eminent holiness, having become acquainted with him when he came to Rome with his father in the time of Clement VIII. Out of devotion he took some of his relics away with him, and wishing to leave some further mark of the love he bore him, he entreated the Pope to allow the fathers of the Congregation of the Oratory to celebrate the Mass, and say the Office of the Blessed Philip. The Pope lent a willing ear to his request, and ordered Cardinal Domenico Pinelli to lay the matter before the Sacred Congregation of Rites. This having been done, on the 10th of January, 1609, the Congregation unanimously agreed that as this was a very grave matter, and, as it were, a private canonization, he should first speak with his holiness, from whom they then procured a Brief directed to the said Congregation, empowering them to revise and consider afresh the first Process, which had been made with the ordinary authority, and also giving them faculties to form the other Processes with apostolic authority, tam in genere quam in specie, as well in Rome as elsewhere.

At this time fresh entreaties were made for the canonization of Philip by different princes and potentates of Christendom; by Louis XIII the most Christian king of France, by Mary de' Medici his mother, by the illustrious senate and people of Rome, by Ferdinand I, Grand Duke of Tuscany, and after his death by Cosimo his son, by Maximilian, Duke of Bavaria, by Charles Gonzaga, Duke of Nevers, of whom we have just spoken, and by Catherine of Lorraine his wife, and also by the Congregation. The Pope assented, and by an Apostolic Brief, dated 13th April, 1609, committed the cause to the Sacred Congregation of Rites. On the 9th of May, in the same year, the Congregation ordered that the second Process, which is called "in genere," should be made, and appointed Cardinal Girolamo Panfilio, the Pope's vicar, to undertake it. This Process was finished and presented to the Congregation on the 20th of June the same year, by whom it was committed to Cardinal Robert Bellarmine to read, and after having well considered it, to report whether they could lawfully proceed and form the third Process, which is called "in specie." He performed his task with all diligence, and the Congregation passed a decree accordingly on the 26th of June, 1609, and Cardinal Domenico Pinello, Bishop of Ostia, and head of the Sacred Congregation, made a full report of the proceedings to Paul V.

The second Process, which, as we have said, is called "in genere," having been made on the 14th of August, in the same year, the Sacred Congregation decreed that the third Process which is called "in specie," should be formed. But since it was considered right that the said Process should be formed by three auditors of the Rota, as had been done in the canonization of S. Francesca and S. Charles, the Pope, by a new rescript of the 7th of July, 1610, committed the cause to three auditors of the Rota, namely, to Francesca Pegna Decano, Orazio Lancellotto, and Dionisio Simone di Marcomonte, who was Archbishop of Lyons and afterwards Cardinal; ordering that either all or at least two of them should form the said Process "in specie," granting them letters remissorial and compulsory to examine and form Processes as well in Rome as out of it for the canonization of Philip. Towards the end of the Process Orazio Lancellotte was made cardinal, and Alessandro Lodovisi was therefore substituted in his place, who himself was afterwards made Cardinal and Archbishop of Bologna, and eventually was assumed to the Pontificate under the name of Gregory XV. On the 19th July, 1610, the said auditors began to form the Process in the sacristy of San Luigi de' Francesi.

This third Process, called "in specie," having been completed with all the necessary formalities, and the Processes that had been drawn up out of Rome having also been brought to a conclusion, fresh entreaties being also made by the above-mentioned princes and potentates, on the 4th of October, 1612, a summary account of the said Processes was laid before the Pope Paul V, by Cardinal Alessandro Lodovisi, Archbishop of Bologna, who still held the office of Auditor of the Rota, and Dionisio Simone Marcomonte, Archbishop of Lyons. The Pope sent their report to the Sacred Congregation of Rites, and they on the 20th of November, in the same year, again referred the cause to Cardinal Bellarmine in order that with the aid of the advocate Giovan Battista Spada, Fiscal Procurator and Promoter of the Faith, he might diligently examine the report which had been made to Paul V, and at the same time the Processes were exhibited to all the cardinals of the Congregation, in order that they might with the greater exactness test the truth and sincerity of the report. This having been done, the said Congregation in eight sittings at different times between the 5th of June, 1614, to the 14th of April, 1615, finally resolved that there was full and sufficient evidence of the validity of the Processes and of the miracles and virtues of the servant of God, Philip Neri.

After this a report was carried to the Pope, showing that the Congregation of the Oratory desired leave to recite the Office and to say the Mass of the said servant of God; and the Pope ordered the Sacred

Congregation of Rites to consider what it was expedient to do in the case. On the 9th of May, 1615, the Sacred Congregation made a decree, declaring that the prayer of the fathers of the Oratory might be granted, and Cardinal Antonio Maria Gallo, then head of the said Congregation of Rites, made a report accordingly to the Pope. He, therefore, in a secret Consistory on the 11th of May in the same year, by the unanimous vote of the cardinals, confirmed this decree of the Sacred Congregation, and on the 25th of the same month, as appears by the brief of that date, the same Pope, Paul V, declared by apostolic authority, that Philip was of the number of the Blessed; at the same time he granted permission to the fathers of the Oratory to recite the Office and say the Mass of the Blessed Philip, and this permission was also granted to all who might be present at their church. In the following year this permission was extended to other Congregations of the Oratory, out of Rome, as appears by an Apostolic Brief, dated the 19th of March, 1616. In the year 1621, Gregory XV granted in addition a perpetual plenary indulgence to all who should devoutly visit the church of the Vallicella on the day of his feast.

After the death of Paul V, Gregory XV was raised to the Pontificate, and the Congregation of the Oratory, and many of the princes already mentioned, and in particular the Roman and Florentine cardinals, made fresh entreaties that he would be pleased to carry on and complete the canonization of Philip. The Pope, therefore, who had himself a particular affection for Philip, on the 22nd of May, in the year 1621, committed the cause again to the Sacred Congregation of Rites, who, on the 10th of July in the same year, appointed Cardinal Robert Bellarmine, to propose the first doubt upon the validity of the processes that had already been made, and on the 7th of August following, this doubt having been accurately examined and discussed, with the assistance of Giovan Battista Spada, Advocate of the Consistory, as Promoter of the Faith, the Congregation resolved unanimously that there was ample evidence of the validity of the Processes.

After this, Cardinal Bellarmine proposed the second doubt, namely, whether from the Processes which had now been several times revised and approved as valid, they might rightly conclude that the sanctity of Philip was sufficiently proved, so that he might be canonized. Three Congregations were held upon this doubt, the first on the 4th of September, 1621, in which it was resolved that there was sufficient evidence of the report of Philip's sanctity, and sufficient evidence of his virtues "in genere" and "in specie" of Faith, Hope, and Charity. On the 17th of September, in the same year, Cardinal Bellarmine was taken from this world to a better, Cardinal Pietro Paolo Crescenzio was therefore appointed in his place; and on the 25th of the same month the second Congregation was held, in which it was likewise resolved, that there was sufficient evidence "in specie" of the other virtues and gifts, as for example, Humility, Virginity, the gift of Prophecy, of Perseverance, &c. The third and last Congregation was held on the 13th of November, in which it was declared that the miracles mentioned in the Processes were fully proved, and consequently that the sanctity of Philip was established, and that he might deservedly be canonized and inscribed among the number of the Saints. The proceedings of the said Congregations having been terminated, a report of them was made to the Pope. His Holiness had for some time past determined to canonize the Blessed Isidore Agricola, and now great entreaties were made that he would canonize at the same time the Blessed Ignatius, Xavier, Theresa, and Philip. The Pope therefore charged the Sacred Congregation of Rites to consider whether it would be well and expedient to canonize these five at the same time. The Congregation in two sittings, held on the 22nd of December, 1621, and the 3rd of January, 1622, respectively, resolved, that if it pleased his Holiness he could and might canonize them all five together, and that it would be more expedient to do it in this manner than to canonize them one by one. On receiving the report of this resolution the Pope greatly rejoiced.

It is the custom of the Holy Roman Church to hold three Consistories before coming to the act of canonization, in order that all the cardinals and prelates who have to give their votes may be fully informed of the case. The first of these is called *secret*, the second *public*, and the third *semi-public*. As the Sacred Congregation of Rites had now declared that it would be advisable to canonize all the five at the same time, the usual Consistories were therefore summoned. On the 19th of January, 1622, the first secret Consistory was held, in which Cardinal Francesco Maria, the head of the Sacred Congregation, presented the report for the canonization of the Blessed Isidore, Ignatius, and Xavier, a printed copy of which was given to all the cardinals. On the twenty-fourth of the same month the secret Consistory was held for the canonization of the Blessed Theresa and Philip, and the report was presented by the same cardinal, and a printed copy of it was likewise given to each cardinal; by this means the Sacred College was well informed of all the particulars of the case before them, and seeing that all the necessary conditions for the canonization of the Saints had been exactly complied with, they decided that if it seemed fit to his Holiness he might proceed to canonize them.

On the 27th of January, in the same year, the second Consistory, which is called *public*, was held for the canonization of the Blessed Isidore Agricola, Ignatius, and Xavier, at which Fausto Caffarelli, Consistorial Advocate and Vicar of the Chapter of S. Peter's, made the Latin oration for the Blessed Isidore; and Niccolò Zambecarri, Consistorial Advocate and Secretary to the Congregation of Bishops, made the oration for the Blessed Ignatius and Xavier.

On the 1st of February, the *public* Consistory for the canonization of the Blessed Theresa and Philip was held, at which Giovan Battista Mellino, Consistorial Advocate, made the accustomed oration for the Blessed Theresa; and Giovan Battista Spada, then coadjutor of his uncle Spada, the Consistorial Advocate, and afterwards cardinal, made the oration for the Blessed Philip; to each of which Giovanni Ciampoli, Secretary of Briefs to Princes, replied in the name of his Holiness, as he had done to the others. At the end, the Pope exhorted all the cardinals and prelates by almsgiving, fasting, and prayer to invoke the assistance of God, in order that His Divine Majesty might be pleased to direct him to that which would be to the greater glory and profit of Holy Church.

The third and last Consistory, which is called *semi-public*, was held for the Blessed Ignatius and Xavier on the 6th of February, and on the twenty-eighth of the same month, for the Blessed Theresa and Philip, at which there were present thirty-two cardinals, one patriarch, nine archbishops, and eighteen bishops, together with some protonotaries, the Auditors of the Rota and the Procurator Fiscal. The doors being closed, his Holiness delivered a short and pious discourse with reference to the matter concerning which they were assembled, after which the votes were taken, and it was agreed that his Holiness might deservedly canonize the five. The Pope therefore, with the advice and consent of the aforesaid voters in two Consistories, determined to canonize them, and having exhorted all to have recourse to almsgiving, fasting, and prayer, he declared his intention to celebrate the canonization on the Feast of S. Gregory the Great, the twelfth of March, 1622; on which day with the applause of all Philip was inscribed, together with the other four, in the number of the Saints, in the church of S. Peter, and with the usual ceremonies.

The decree of the canonization having been promulgated, and the ceremonies employed by the Church on these occasions having been performed, the hymn Te Deum Laudamus was solemnly sung, and the assistance of God having been sought through the intercession of the five Saints, the Supreme Pontiff recited a prayer in common to all five, and then celebrated solemn mass at the altar of the apostles. He also granted a plenary indulgence to all who having confessed and communicated were present at that function.

The same evening a Capuchin was praying in the chapel where Philip's body was lying, when suddenly the newly canonized Saint appeared to him, as it were, in triumph; his face was of exceeding beauty, and he was clothed in a rich mantle; he was attended by a holy company who stood round him in a circle. The religious was not in the least alarmed, but taking confidence from the kindness which appeared in the countenance of the aged Saint, he ventured to ask him what was the meaning of that illustrious suite that accompanied him. The Saint with a benignant smile told him that it was composed of the fathers and brethren of the Oratory, and of seculars who had followed his holy institute, and had frequented his holy exercises, and that among them were five who were not members of the Congregation, but brothers of the little Oratory, all of whom he had that day liberated from Purgatory by his intercession, and he was now conducting them to Paradise. He also charged him to tell the fathers and brothers of the Congregation, and also the secular brethren of the little Oratory, that they were to observe in all things the holy institute he had left them, for that it was pleasing to the Divine Majesty that the fathers should treat all alike, both rich and poor, and that both the fathers and the lay-brothers should be treated in the same way, because they were all his children; he likewise ordered him to tell them for their consolation, that up to that day, by the grace of God, not one of the Congregation who had died had been lost, but each one had been saved. Another Capuchin on the following Sunday saw the picture of the Saint over the altar of the Oratory raise his hand and bless the Congregation and all the brethren of the Oratory.

The devotion to S. Philip rapidly spread through all Christendom; in many cities of Italy and elsewhere there were grand festivals and processions in honor of him. In Spain in particular, in the city of Madrid, at the procession of the Five Saints, Elizabeth, the Queen of Spain, with her own hands adorned the statue of Philip with a beautiful chasuble richly decked with diamonds. Pope Urban VIII granted the Office of S. Philip as a semi-double ad libitum to the whole Church; Innocent X made it of precept; and Clement IX, in 1669 raised it to a double of precept for the whole Church. Alexander VIII granted the proper mass for the Saint for the whole Church, and Benedict XIV in 1745 approved of the proper office of the Saint for the kingdom of Portugal, and it has since been extended to many congregations and dioceses. Altars and churches have been erected in his honor in many places, and many have chosen him as their advocate and protector. The Dominican fathers have decreed that throughout their order his feast is to be observed as a double; and Clement IX from his singular devotion towards the Saint, on the 8th of June, 1669, ordered that for the future the Feast of S. Philip should be observed throughout the Catholic Church. Many cities have also ordained that his Feast shall be observed yearly as a feast appointed by the Church. Meantime the goodness of God was continually co-operating towards the increase of this devotion by the many miracles and graces which He bestowed on those who in any way recommended themselves to the intercession of the Saint, as will be related at the end of the Sixth Book. Finally, Benedict XIII, out of gratitude to the Saint for the singular favors he had received from him, especially for his miraculous preservation by the Saint in an earthquake, as we shall relate hereafter, commanded in 1726 that his Feast should be observed in Rome as of precept.

Thus, what the Saint had often foretold in his lifetime was fully verified; for he used to say, "You will one day see my body treated with the same honor that the bodies of the Saints are treated with, and you will see votive offerings sent to my tomb." On another occasion, when he was asked to go to Florence, at least to see his native town again, he replied, "I shall be tied up at Florence;" the meaning of these words was not understood till his standard was fixed up in the church of Santa Maria del Fiore in that city. Indeed, like another S. Peter, he promised some of his friends that he would pray for them after he had left his earthly tabernacle, telling them frequently that they might be certain that although he was dead he had gone to a place where he could render them much greater assistance. He also promised some of his friends that he would be present at their death; he made this promise in particular to Costanza del Drago, saying, "Do not fear, do not fear, I will never abandon you; I will do for you what S. Francis and S. Clare have done for those devoted to them."

Printed in Great Britain
by Amazon

41579380R00098